4⁰⁰

The Canadian Canoe

The Canadian Canoe

by
H. R. Gardner

Illustrated
by
Brian L. Stone

ISBN 0-88839-243-5

Cataloging in Publication Data
H. R. Gardner, 1927-
The Canadian Canoe

ISBN 0-88839-243-5

1. Canoes and canoeing—Canada. I. Title
GV776.15.A2G37 1994 797.1'22'0971 C94-910740-97

Printed in Canada-Hignell

Copy edit: Barbara Brown
Production: Jeffrey R. Stilz
Cover painting: Brian L. Stone

Published simultaneously in Canada and the United States by

HANCOCK HOUSE PUBLISHERS LTD.
19313 Zero Avenue, Surrey, B.C. V4P 1M7
(604) 538-1114 Fax (604) 538-2262

HANCOCK HOUSE PUBLISHERS
1431 Harrison Avenue, Blaine, WA 98230-5005
1-800-938-1114 Fax (604) 538-2262

Contents

To Robin,
who should have written this.

Acknowledgments

Several people have contributed substantially to making this book possible, and I would like to thank them.

My wife Kay, the Honourable Stanton Hogg, my daughter Kathi, Dr. E. M. Hagmeier, Dr. G. W. S. Brodsky, Mr. D. H. Keen, and Mr. B. L. Stone.

And finally, Mr. R. L. (Robin) Hepburn, who taught me almost everything I know about the subject.

He was young, fit, athletic, and an experienced canoeist. One day, he had occasion to paddle across the river, against a fairly strong headwind.

As he set out, in a new, modern, canvas canoe, an old Indian woman departed simultaneously, presumably for the same destination. She appeared to be in her late sixties or seventies, under 100 pounds in weight, and paddling an old bark canoe, badly misshapen, with several broken ribs.

His initial reaction was to "show her how a canoe should be paddled," but he soon had cause to reassess the situation. In spite of every effort he could make, to the point of approaching total exhaustion at the trip's end, he found that not only could he not win this "race," he could not even keep up with her, and fell farther and farther behind.

Introduction

For almost half a century, I have been an avid boater, and notwithstanding occasional forays into power and sail, the canoe has always been my first love. I do not canoe here on Vancouver Island because to me it is not canoe country.

When in Rome, do as the Romans do, so here I sail. Nevertheless, when we came West I brought two canvas canoes, ever hopeful. After they sat on trestles in the back yard for two years, I disposed of them, reluctantly.

Many years ago, as a young soldier, I lived on the Moehne Talsperre in Westphalia, Germany. It was one of the few lakes in that part of the world (man-made) and therefore in season attracted a large camping and boating public. The boats were almost exclusively European canoes, similar to what we would call a kayak.

One day, however, I saw a familiar shape and, unable to contain myself, hurried to make the acquaintance of the owner. With some difficulty, I made known to him the reason for my forwardness. He, somewhat relieved to discover I was only interested in his boat, said *"Ah, das Kanadische kanu. Bitte, mein Herr"* (or something like that). This invitation I accepted gratefully, and off I went for a paddle.

Until then I had not realized that internationally this boat was known as the *Canadian Canoe*.

Altogether, I suppose I have paddled fifty different canoes: several of my own, several belonging to friends, and the balance rented from outfitters. Most were canvas covered, some fiberglass, and some aluminum. They ranged from twelve to twenty feet in length, fifty to one hundred and twenty pounds in weight (not including my twenty-foot square stern freighter), and in condition ranging from excellent to poor.

Six of us and a large dog enjoyed tripping in two fifteen-foot canvas canoes, complete with tents, sleeping gear, grub, utensils, dog chow, and bug lotion. I use the term "enjoy" without apology, because, in retrospect, all agree the experiences were enjoyable, although at the time, children being what they are, they sometimes had to be told they were enjoying themselves.

Sixteen or seventeen-foot canoes might have been more appropriate, but since I had to do all the canoe carrying, I preferred the lighter fifteens.

We had no problems. The three older ones paddled one boat, and Mom and I had the other with dog and the youngest.

Vacation time, in those days, consisted of heading North with two canoes on top and the little twelve upturned on the motor canoe, which was trailered. Everyone had his own paddle, and was expected to use it, even in the big canoe.

I read that there is a tremendous revival of interest in canoeing today, and my observations would tend to confirm this. Even here on the Island, one vehicle in twenty-five has a canoe on top, and many more can be seen in backyards.

What disturbs me is that the boats I see only vaguely resemble canoes in design, and the performance of the paddlers I have managed to observe, be it in local waters or on international TV, suggests something is dreadfully wrong with the "state of the art."

I am not a hidebound purist or traditionalist. Good boating to me is safe, efficient, sensible boating, irrespective of the mode, be it power, sail, canoe, or whatever. With few provisos, I acknowledge the superiority of modern materials over ribs, planks, and canvas. If the manufacturer produces a satisfactory product and the boater learns his part, it makes for better boating all around, and everyone benefits.

My message is that I don't think this is happening. As for the manufacturer, I recognize entrepreneurism is more likely to be the name of his game than promotion of good canoeing; nevertheless, unless the consumer is well enough informed to tell him his product is unsatisfactory, nothing will change.

The myth that all Canadians are born with an innate ability to handle a canoe is patently ridiculous; nevertheless, it would appear some of this inanity exists. The number of people who would unhesitatingly take driving, swimming, golf, tennis, banjo, and dog obedience lessons from an expert, but who purchase the most dangerous, unstable, demanding, and inefficient watercraft available, and proceed to use it with no knowledge or instruction, boggles the mind.

Furthermore, in the literature about canoeing, there is far more romantic drivel than fact. The myth and romance of the canoe is not to be denied, but with apologies to Pauline Johnson, creator of "The Song My Paddle Sings," your paddle won't sing any songs if the boat you have doesn't perform like a canoe, and you yourself have not bothered to learn the art of paddling.

1

The Boat

What Is A Canoe?

Canoe, Carib Ind., Spanish; Canôt, Fr.—a small boat propelled by paddles.

A century ago, there were hundreds of canoe clubs along the Eastern seaboard, in the St. Lawrence, in the Great Lakes, and in all the lakes and waterways of this established, populated "world." If one wanted to get involved in organized boating, that is, cruising or racing, there were two choices: yacht clubs or canoe clubs.

I have bound issues of the periodical *Field and Stream* published in New York for the years 1883 and 1884. No small part of these publications is devoted to canoe clubs, their correspondence, activities, and thoughts on design and performance of canoes. Muskoka and Haliburton are as well-represented as New York, Toronto, or Nantucket.

It was apparent even then, however, that these clubs

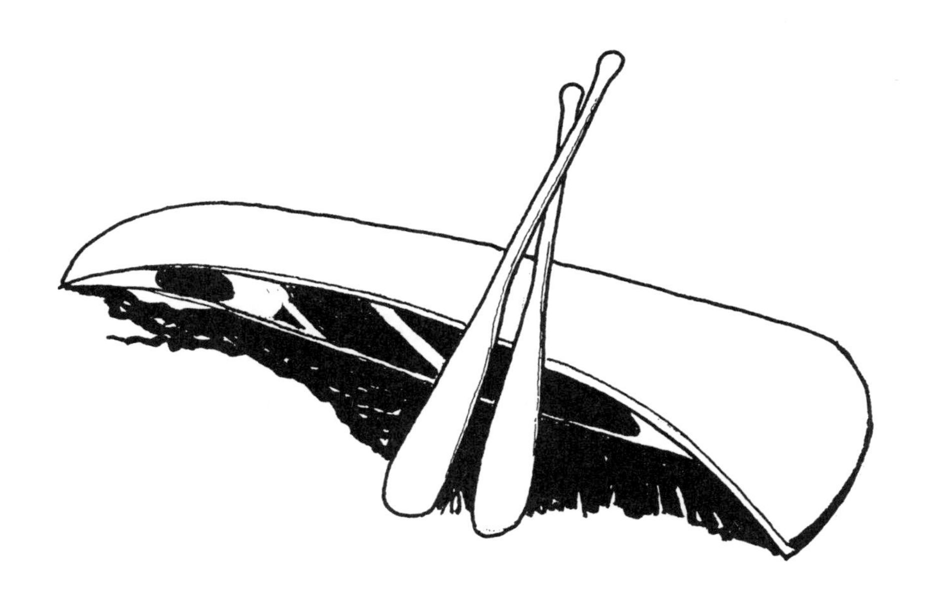

were following a definite trend that eventually would produce the sailing dinghy as we know it today.

Their canoes were European canoes, and, although paddling and carrying were considerations in cruising, the emphasis was primarily on sailing characteristics. Classes of "canoes" were apparent then too: Rob Roy, Stella Maris, Barnegat Bay Sneak Box, etc., some of which later became identified as dinghies.

Over the years, paddling became less and less important, and portability was sacrificed entirely for sail performance. Today, there are still canoe clubs perpetuating that era, but they are primarily yacht or dinghy clubs, with the occasional concession of a racing canoe component in their membership. Very seldom did the members of these clubs consider the Canadian canoe a satisfactory hull for their purpose.

Another type of canoeing, to be classified with sport parachuting, hang gliding, and mountain climbing, white-water canoeing is to cruising or pleasure canoeing what Le Mans formula racing is to Sunday afternoon driving. It is definitely not a form of transportation and requires highly specialized equipment and techniques. That is not to say a Canadian canoe might not do a white-water run in the course of a canoe trip, but portage is invariably a preferable alternative, and an open, undecked boat is a poor white-water boat.

Until fifty years ago, the Canadian canoe was the undisputed master of Northern transportation. Parties whose destination might be hundreds or even thousands of miles into the hinterlands cherished every fraction of a knot of speed they could attain, every ounce that did not have to be carried, and each characteristic that might ease or hasten the journey. There are many documented cases of parties refusing to set out unless provided with the canoe they preferred, usually a Chestnut.

With the advent of the bush plane, all this changed. If the only requirement was to paddle a few miles after the aircraft had lifted boat and paddlers over hundreds of miles, what mattered a little compromise in equipment and technique?

Compared to most boats, the Canadian canoe is cramped, unstable, unseaworthy, slow, fragile, etc., etc. Why, then, does it exist?

Several characteristics uniquely suit it for travel in the North:

1. it can be manoeuvred through narrow, tortuous, or weed-clogged waterways;
2. it will float on a wet handkerchief;
3. when it can no longer be floated, one can pick it up and carry it.

And that's it! If you don't need those characteristics, there is a better boat for your purpose. Almost any boat is better than a canoe—except when you need those characteristics. Then nothing else will do!

New Boats For Old

Primitive man, faced with the need for water transportation, evolved many ingenious solutions to the problem. The parameters of his solution were invariably defined by three criteria: the nature of the need (that is, the characteristics of the waterway), materials available, and the state of his technology. In most instances, the materials and technology dictated a solution that was, at best, a compromise.

With few exceptions (for example, the moose-hide bullboat of the Arctic Indians), the advent of modern materials and technology has produced better alternatives whose superiority is so apparent it overrides the strong traditionalism of primitive peoples. No Athapaskan would choose the traditional bark canoe with high prow and stern over a modern motorboat or motorcanoe for use in the big lakes of the Arctic. No Nootka would consider fishing from a dugout today, not when he can use a modern trawler or seiner.

This is not the case with the Canadian canoe as developed by the Algonkian tribes of the North East. Primarily a design conceptualized and developed to near perfection by the Woodland Cree, Montagnais, and Ojibway tribes, it is still the only form of transportation ideally suited to the lake-dotted country of the Canadian shield, and this notwithstanding the advent of the STOL Aircraft.

Initially, modern technology and materials contributed a quantum leap in the development of this boat. Although close to perfection in its functional design, the materials available left much to be desired. The boats were extremely fragile, and the skin was rough. Substitution of smooth painted canvas over the planks addressed this problem nicely, and the subsequent advent of plastic and fiberglass held great promise.

So what happened? Where did the plethora of tupperware monstrosities come from, which only vaguely resemble the canoe, and do not perform in any way like a canoe?

The only way to answer these questions is to examine in detail the desirable characteristics of the canoe, and although the Indians developed the canoe without the benefit of the technology of the naval architect, it is within the body of knowledge of his discipline that most of the answers lie.

A Glossary

Abeam — at right angles to the fore and aft centerline.

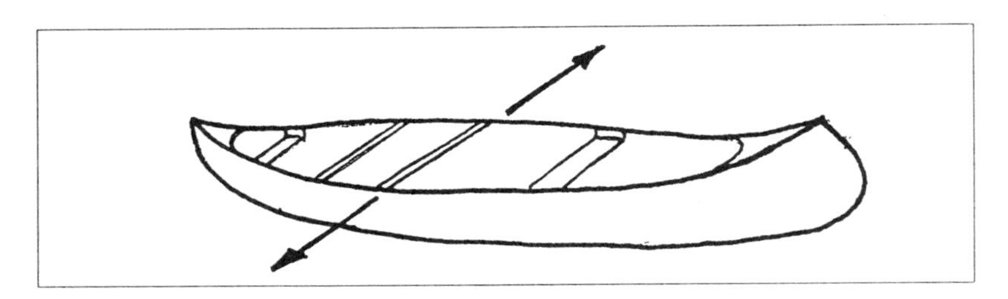

Aft — to the rear or stern.

Angle of Deadrise — the upward slanting of the bottom of the hull from the centerline to the turn of the bilge.

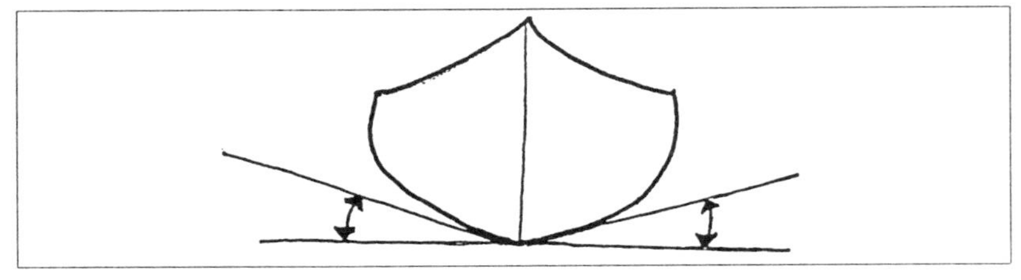

Beam — the width of the hull at its widest part.

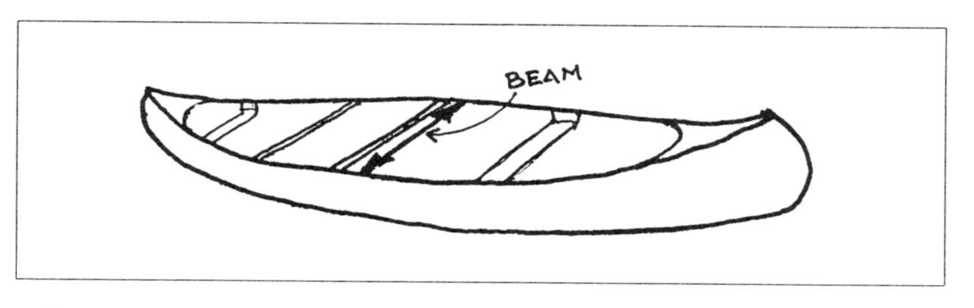

Bilge — where the boat's bottom turns into her topsides on both sides of the hull.

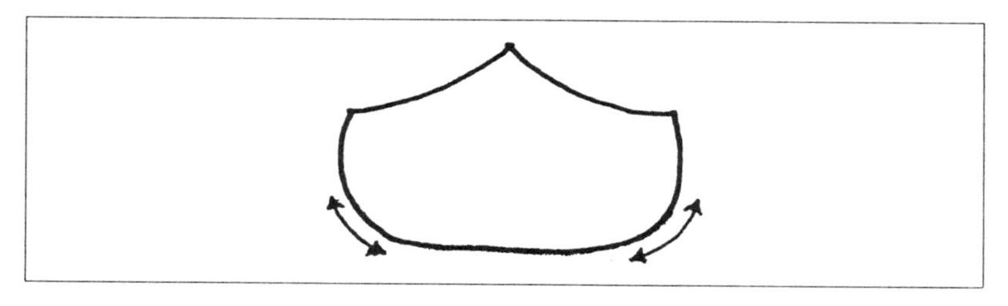

Centre of Gravity — point at which the entire weight of the hull and cargo may be considered as concentrated.

Chine — backbone, or keel line.

Displacement — actual weight Archimedes' Principle: a floating object displaces its own weight in water.

Displacement Hull — a boat hull limited in speed by its own wave system, that is, it cannot plane.

Entry/Exit — the foremost and hindmost points on the hull to enter and leave the water.

Fairbody Draft — depth below the water's surface of the deepest part of the hull. Also known simply as draft.

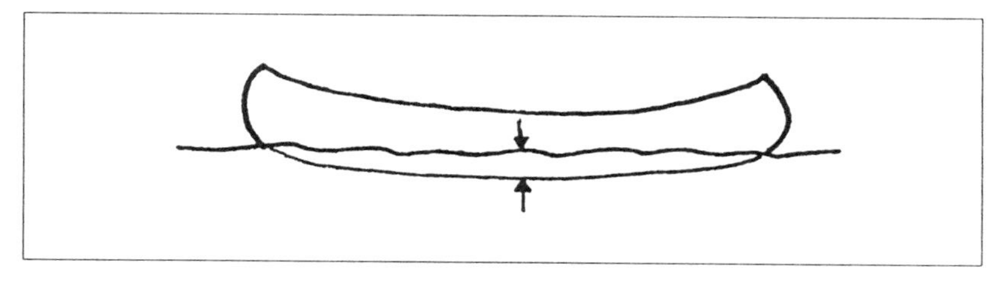

Feathering — movement of the paddle through the water with the edge of the blade forward in a manner to produce the least resistance.

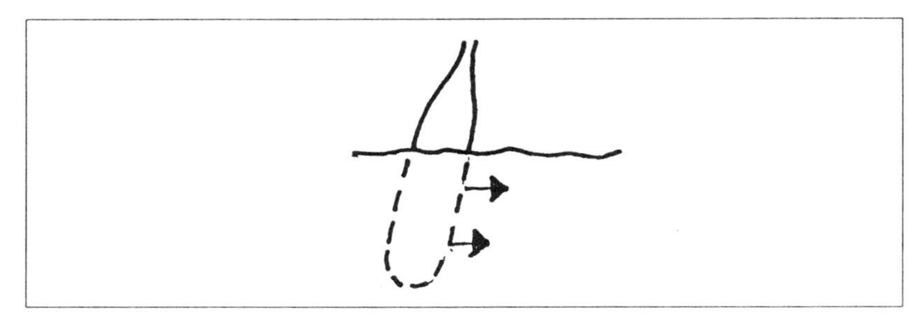

Flare — outward slanting of the topsides.

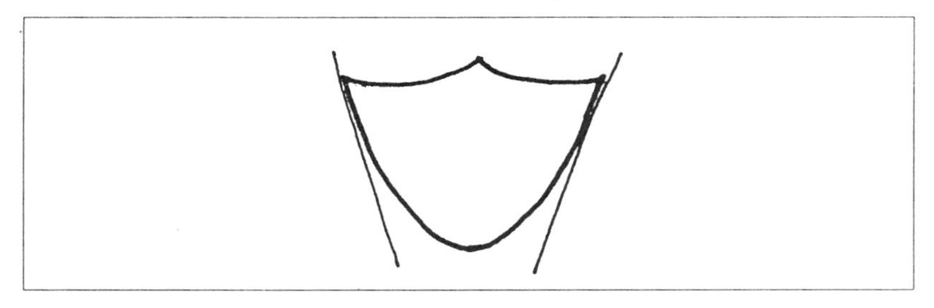

Fore and Aft Centerline — the keel line.

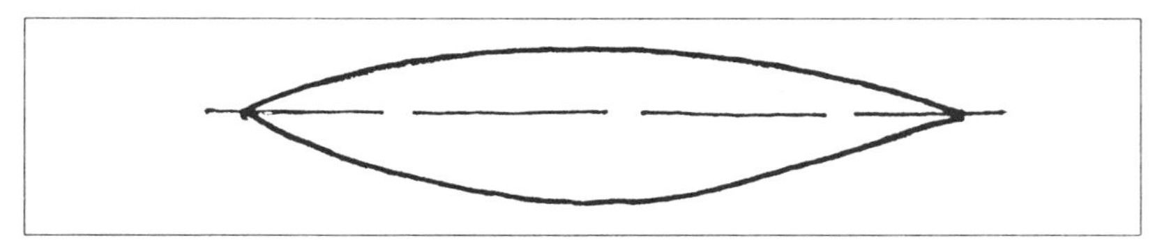

Form Resistance — additional resistance due to formation of eddies or turbulence apart from wave-making.

Freeboard — distance from the water's surface to the gunwale, usually at the gunwale's lowest point.

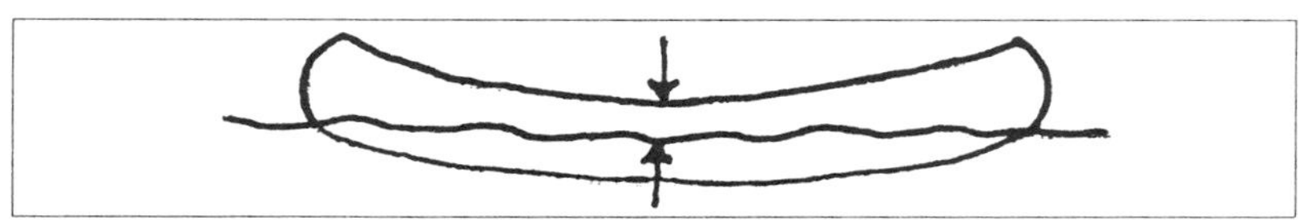

Gunwale — strips of wood or other material that extend along the upper edges of the topsides. An inner strip is called the inwale, and the outer strip is called the outwale.

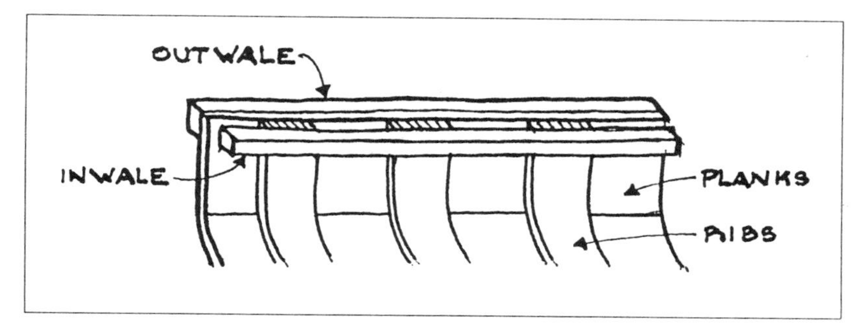

Hard Bilge — makes a sharp, tight turn.

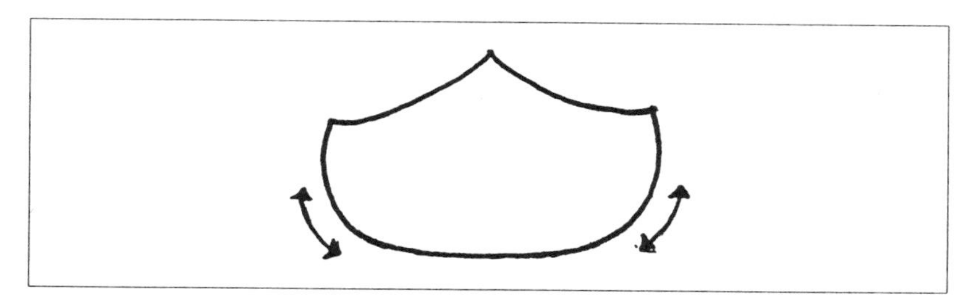

Load Water Line (LWL) — the actual contact of the water's surface and the hull.

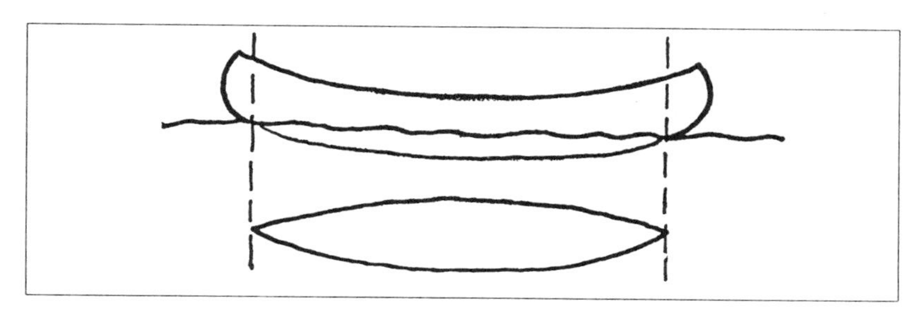

Midship Section — section at midpoint of LWL, usually numbered station #5.

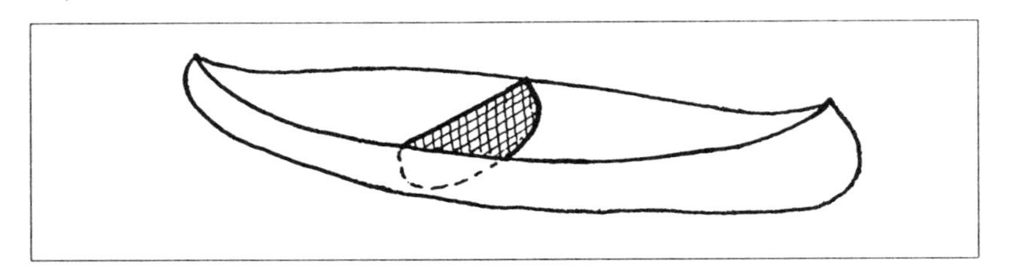

Planking — thin boards covering the outsides of the ribs to form the hull of a wooden boat.

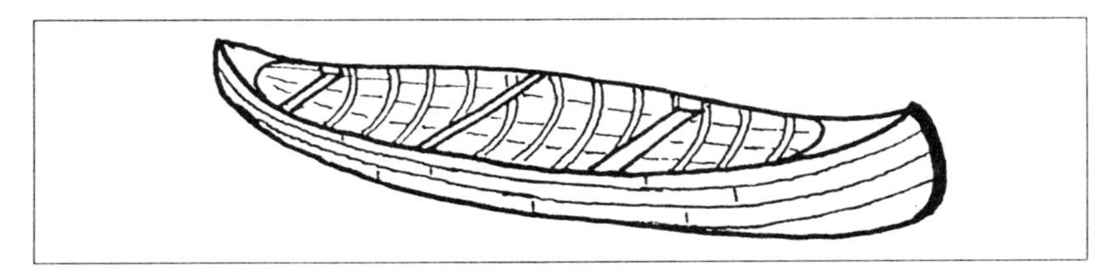

Rocker — the upward sweep of the fore and aft centerline from the center section to the bow and stern.

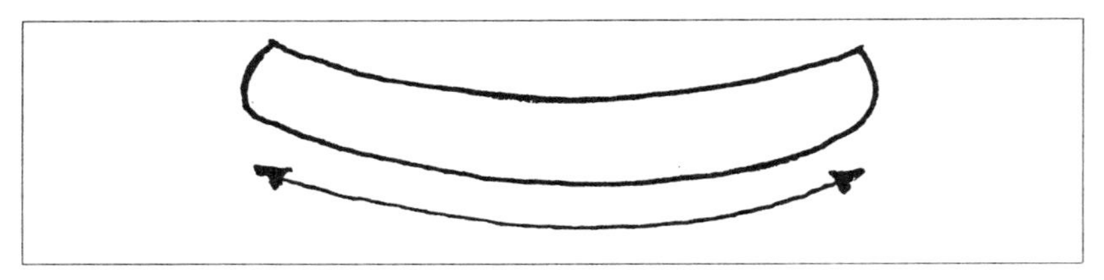

Sections — lines formed by vertical planes passing through the hull at right angles to the fore and aft centerline. Usually divide the LWL into ten equal parts.

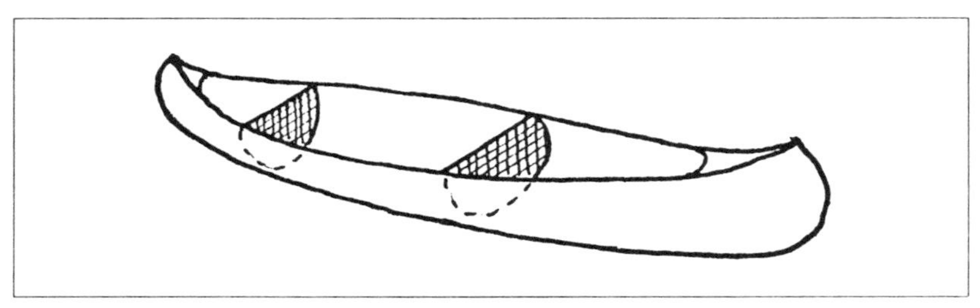

Sheer — the upward sweep of the gunwale towards the bow and stern.

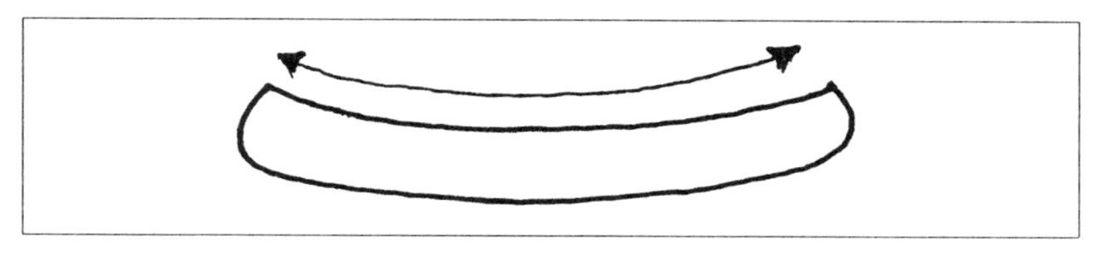

Slack Bilge — makes a slow, gradual turn.

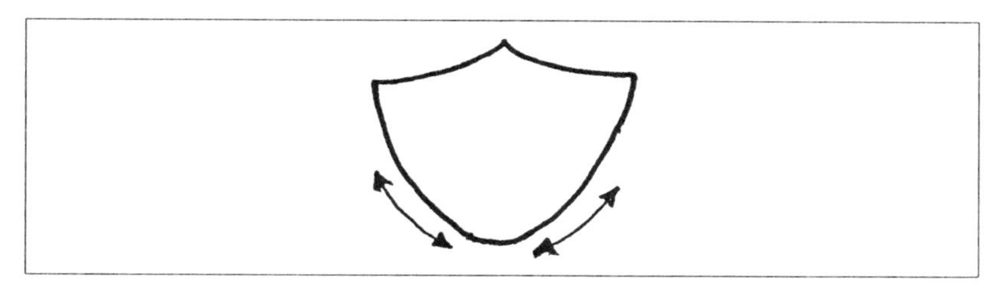

Stability — tendency of a boat to return to upright after being heeled.

Stem — the curved piece of wood etc., which makes the prow or bow.

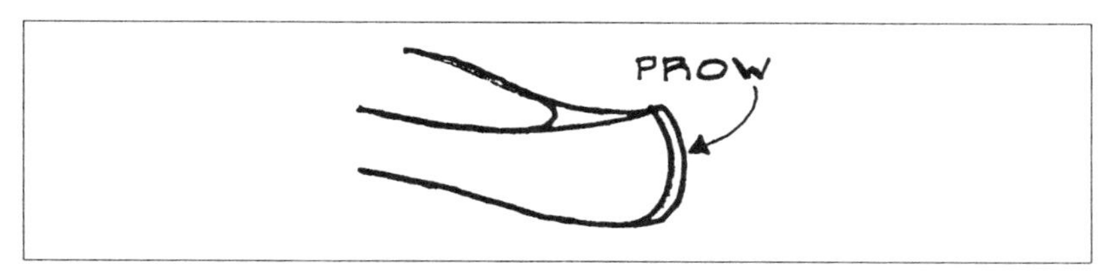

Thwart — a brace of strong wood or metal extending across the top of the canoe from gunwale to gunwale.

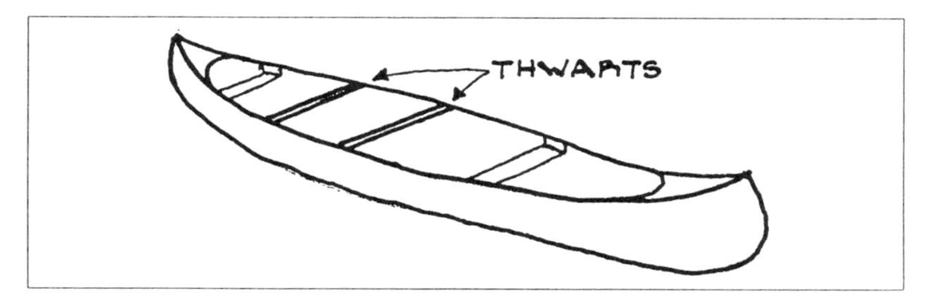

Topside — the sides of the hull above the bilges.

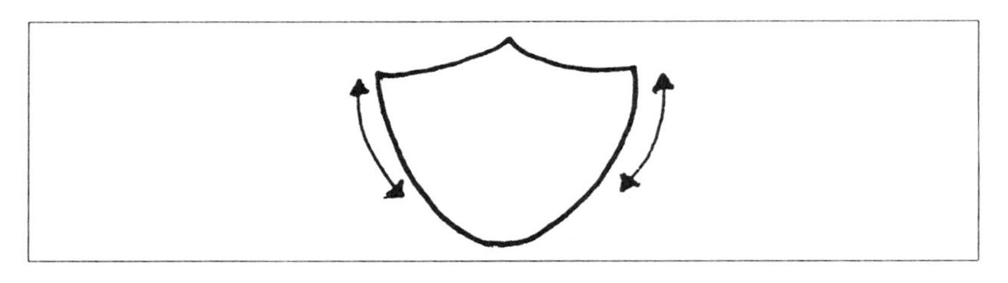

Tumblehome — turning inward of the topsides near the gunwales to produce a narrower beam at the gunwales than below them.

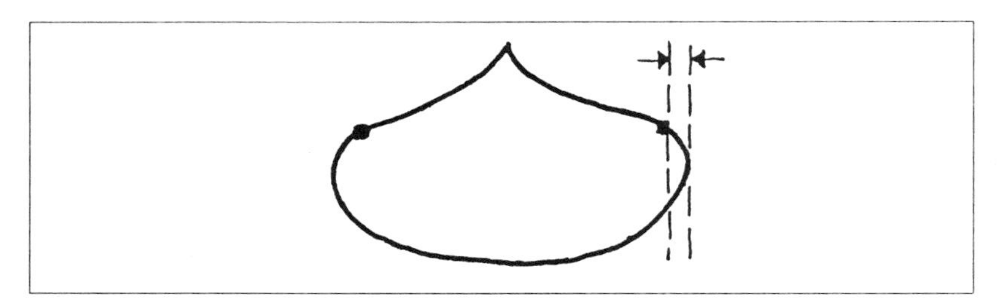

Turn of the Bilge — athwartship curve where the boat's bottom turns into her topsides.

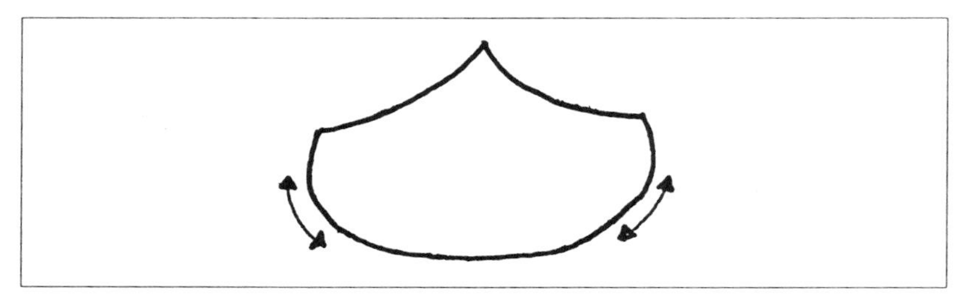

Waterline Configuration — the shape of the hull at the LWL as viewed from above (plan).

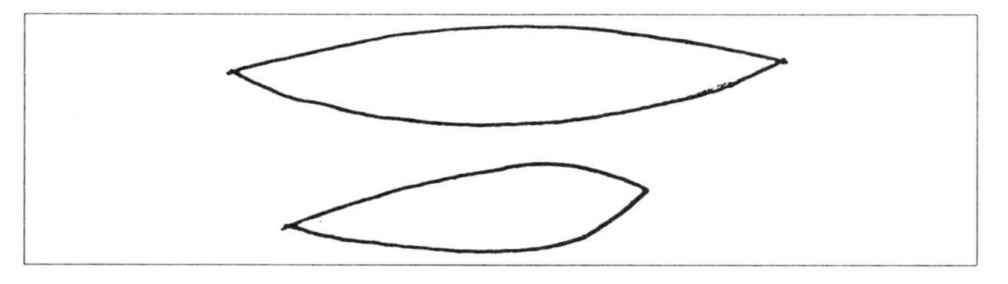

Wave-Making Resistance — waves caused by the hull's forward movement, which become increasingly harmful to speed, the faster the hull moves. Depend on waterline configuration, displacement, and LWL length.

Wetted Surface Resistance — the skin friction between the immersed surface of the hull and the surrounding water.

With Apologies To All Marine Architects

The canoe is a displacement hull, that is, a hull limited in speed by its own wave system, and as such, is subject to several interrelated factors that influence the performance of any displacement hull. These can be grouped under two headings: resistance and axial turning.

Resistance

A hull's forward resistance is the resultant of a number of different drag forces. The relevant ones in the case of a canoe are drag induced by wetted surface, wave propagation, and form resistance.

WETTED SURFACE AREA causes most of the forward resistance or drag at low speed, as a result of the skin friction between the water and the hull's surface.

In actual fact, this drag results from friction between water molecules, called the boundary layer, which cling to the hull's surface and move along with it at the same speed, and water molecules a slight distance away from the hull's surface.

The point to note here is the larger the wetted surface area, the more drag or resistance.

WAVE PROPAGATION is the most important source of drag at higher speeds. As a displacement hull moves forward, it sets up pressure that propagates several wave systems.

These are waves that have their crest line almost at right angles to the direction in which the boat is moving, called transverse waves, and waves that stream backward from the hull at approximately 45 degrees to the direction of motion, called divergent waves.

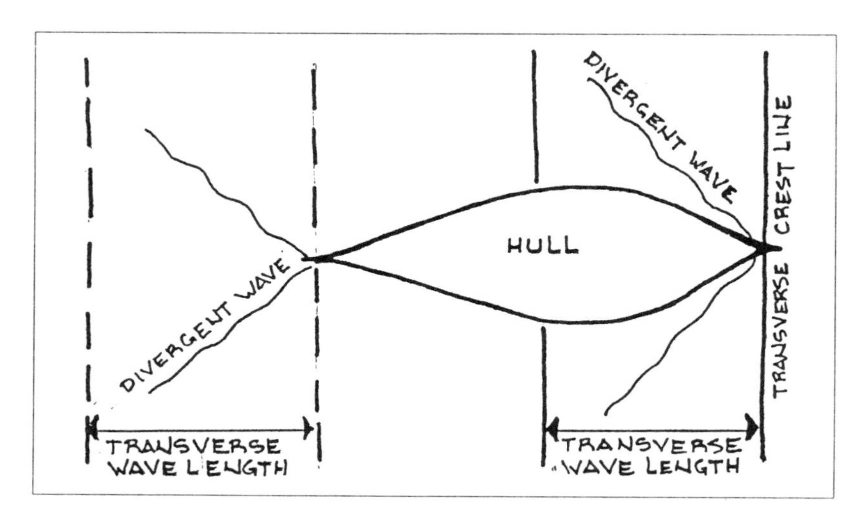

The transverse waves, propagated from the bow and stern simultaneously, move in the same direction as the boat and at approximately the same speed. The faster the speed of the hull, the faster will be the transverse waves, and the longer they will be, because the speed of a wave is proportional to its length from crest to crest.

When the speed of the hull (and therefore the bow wave) is such that the transverse bow wave length corresponds to the load waterline length (LWL), the transverse bow wave reinforces the transverse stern wave, and the drag set up is so substantial that the hull can go no faster without a tremendous expenditure of energy and without planing or behaving in some fashion for which the hull was not designed.

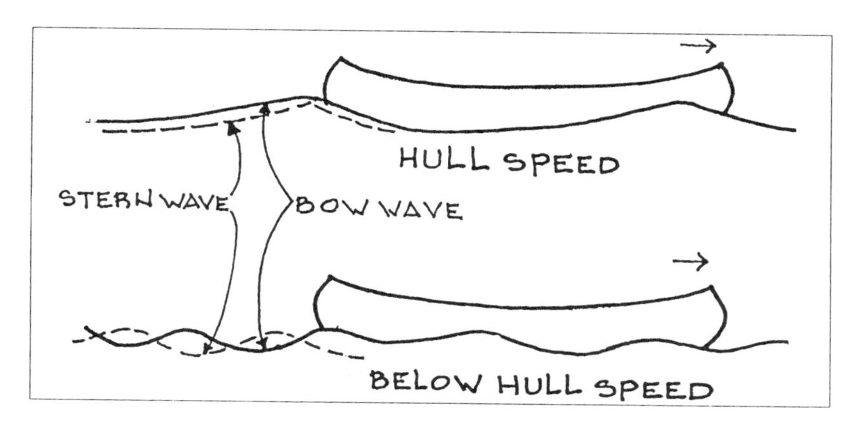

Try towing a canoe behind a motorboat sometime, and you will find at a certain speed the canoe will try to get up and plane. If it happens to be loaded when this happens, it will probably break its back, or at least crumple or tear the hull.

Displacement is also relevant here. A heavily-loaded hull displacing more water, but trimmed with the same LWL as a lighter hull, will nevertheless experience more drag because, although the waves are the same length for a given speed, those of the heavier hull are deeper.

For other boats (for example, sailboats) that closely resemble a canoe in many characteristics, there is a formula used to calculate the theoretical speed of a displacement hull:

speed = 1.3 x square root of LWL

The important point here is not that one can calculate a hull speed, or that longer canoes are faster than shorter canoes (they are!), but that the canoe should be capable of being operated at all times with a maximum waterline length.

If this is significant in the design of sailing hulls, so much so that many sailboats are designed to lengthen their LWL when heeled over, how much more relevant in the case of a canoe, which changes its LWL with each addition or deletion of passengers and cargo, and frequently has only part of the hull immersed?

Now we are between the horns of a dilemma. We wish to maximize the LWL and simultaneously minimize the wetted surface. Are the two mutually exclusive?

Not necessarily! As usual, compromise is the keyword, but here the third factor enters into the calculations.

FORM RESISTANCE from the hull shape is in part inseparable from wave propagation because the sharpness or bluntness of entry into the water at the bow and the exit from the water at the stern will affect the making of waves. In addition, however, the underwater configuration of the hull also plays a part in producing form resistance or drag.

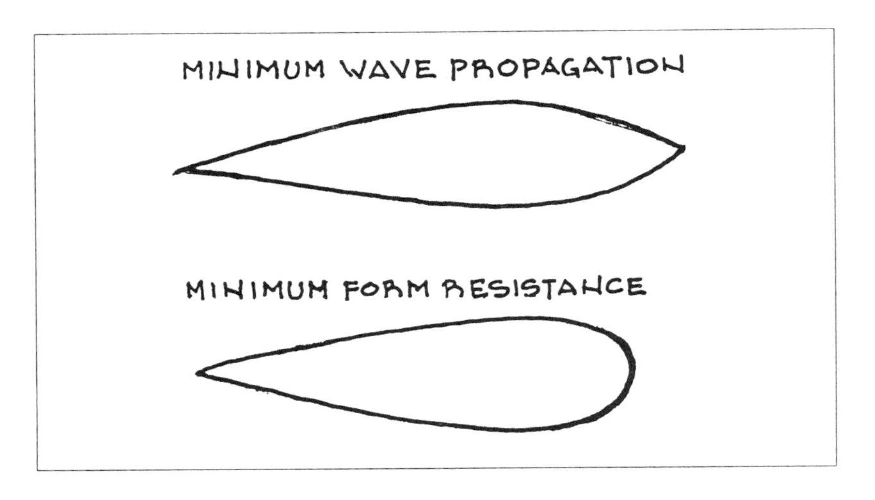

A submarine, while submerged, produces no waves. Therefore, if hull shape were irrelevant, it would be spherical in form, since this configuration produces the smallest wetted surface (area) for a given volume.

In fact, form resistance is a type of drag resulting from the requirement that the hull, moving through the water, must utilize energy to divide the water, or move it aside. This water must also flow around the submerged hull and reunite, and any turbulence or eddies produced in this process will cause resistance or drag.

Whereas a fairly fine entry is desirable at the waterline to minimize wave-making, the underwater configuration at the bow should be relatively coarse. Anyone who has seen the bulbous underwater bow of modern freighters may be aware that the addition of this configuration to a conventional sharp prow adds several knots of speed potential.

Axial Turning

The hull turns around three axes: around the vertical axis for steering control; around the longitudinal axis for stability, for example, rolling, heeling, righting; and around the transverse axis for trim.

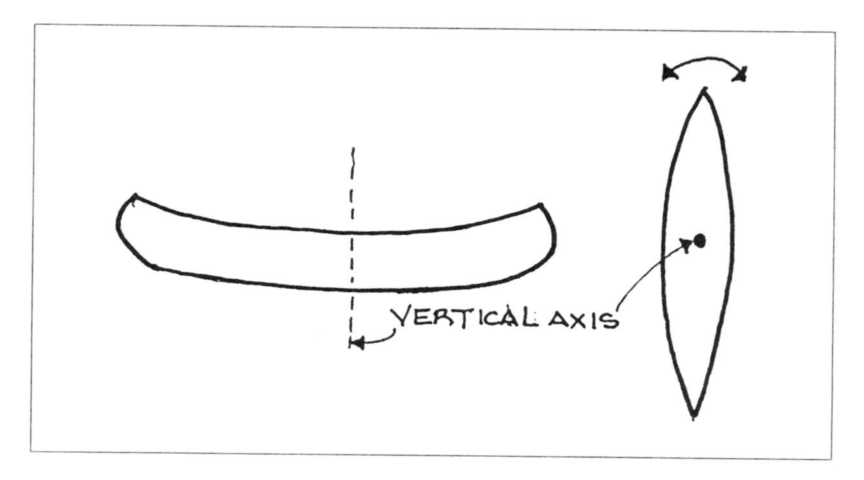

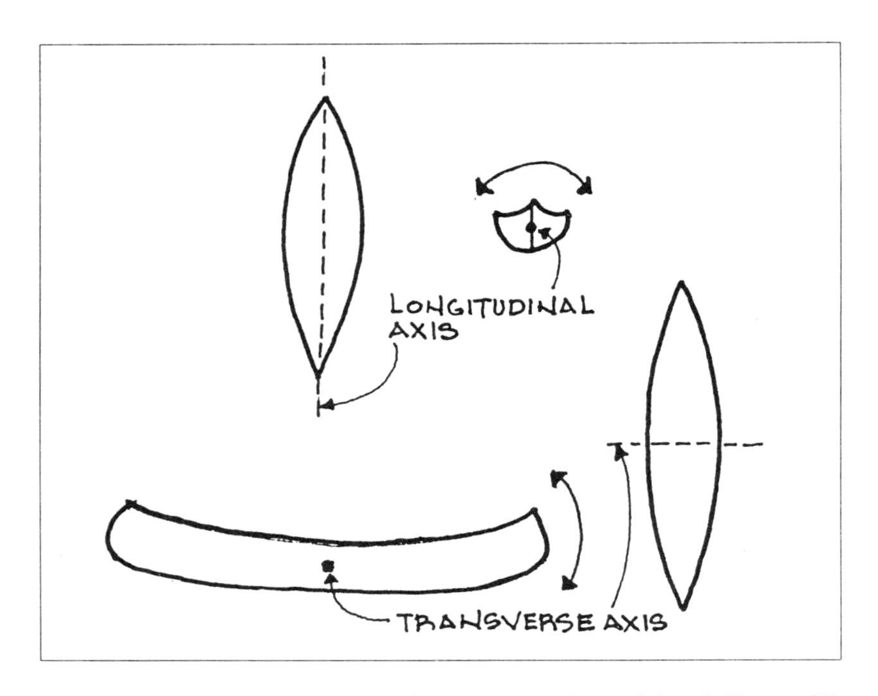

Increase of the LWL without a rockered keel line will reduce the maneuverability, as will the addition of a keel, and thereby affect the turning ability around the vertical axis.

Reduction of the beam, a high deadrise, slack bilges, and flared topsides all contribute to instability around the longitudinal axis.

Improper trim with ballast too far aft where the fine exit has reduced buoyancy will produce instability around the transverse axis.

One might be persuaded that the optimal canoe hull is that of the racing canoe. It has the longest LWL, a good hull shape, and the least wetted surface possible.

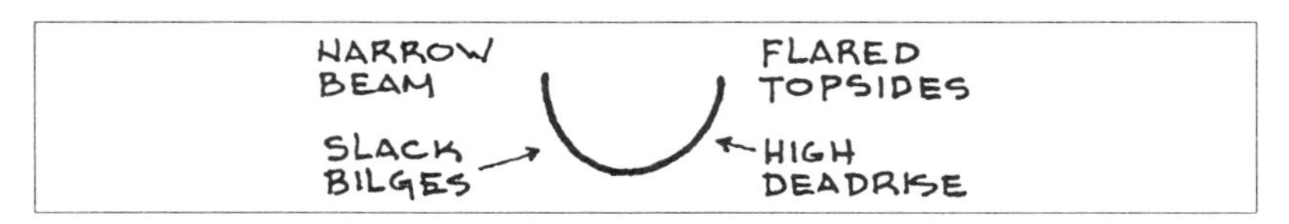

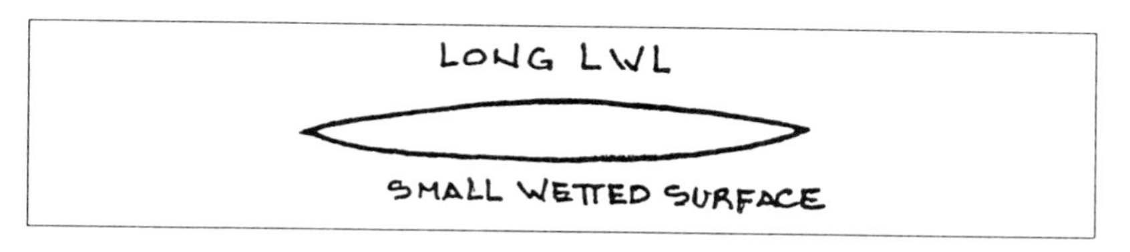

However, it lacks maneuverability, precisely fits the foregoing description of a hull lacking transverse stability, and has no load carrying capability. It is designed to carry one cargo (in one position)—the paddler(s).

It appears we want the following characteristics:

- A maximum LWL
- A minimum wetted area
- A fine entry and exit
- A slightly coarser underwater shape at the bow
- A rockered keel line
- A low deadrise
- A large cargo capacity
- A fairbody draft aft off but near the center of the LWL
- Tumblehome on the topsides
- Stability, particularly on the transverse and longitudinal axes

Notwithstanding the fact that some of the foregoing characteristics are, if not diametrically opposed or mutually exclusive, at least antagonistic to each other, it is quite possible one could, with compromise, proceed to build a satisfactory hull. That is what is done in the design of most boats, but consider this.

A sailing yacht is subject to very little change in cargo or shifting of ballast, except in the repositioning of crew weight, and this is a relatively insignificant fraction of the all-up displacement of the boat. A sailing dinghy is more vulnerable, but seldom carries any cargo except the crew, and that is narrowly defined, for example, one man, two men, etc.

Not so with a canoe. It may be required to carry one man alone, or the same man and 500 pounds of cargo, or two men, or three men, with varying amounts and distribution of cargo. Furthermore, it is just as likely to be propelled stern first as bow first on occasion. How does one design a hull to meet all these conditions?

With difficulty. But the Algonkians did it!

Properly trimmed for the cargo it is carrying, a well-shaped Canadian canoe is capable of producing a waterline configuration with the best possible combination of LWL, wetted surface area, lack of turbulence, and low wave-making potential, whether paddled stern first and empty by one paddler, or gunwales down with two paddlers and several hundred pounds of gear.

As evolved in its birch bark configuration, the canoe has a fine entry and exit, high deadrise, slack bilges, and flared topsides bow and stern, gradually blending in smooth arcs into a low deadrise, sharp bilges, and tumble-homed topsides at the wide beamed center section. The hull had no keel, but was distinctly rockered over the length of its keel line. It was not necessarily symmetrical fore and aft of the center section. The bow half tapers more gradually and symmetrically from the center thwart to the stem, whereas the stern half maintains a wider beam further aft, pinching in to the stern sections more abruptly. The bark skin, being rough, produced a substantial amount of form resistance; however, when smooth canvas was substituted for bark, this ceased to be a problem.

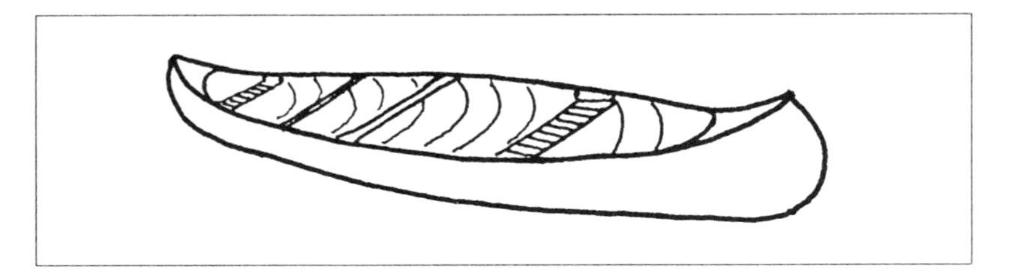

Each of the foregoing design characteristics was interrelated with all of the others in such a fashion that the ideal (or at least the best possible compromise) of waterline and underwater shape or form was realized under any condition of load or trim.

Suppose you were a would-be boat builder. You have a quantity of fiberglass cloth and roving, and some resin, so you set out to build a canoe mould.

Now it's one thing to design a mould incorporating the complex sections as they change from stem and stern to the center thwart, but if in addition it is necessary to rocker the bottom of the hull, the mould, in architectural terms, becomes complex indeed.

How much easier to design a hull with a dead flat keel line, and, incidentally, incorporate a moulded in keel to add strength to the whole structure.

Some of the hulls one sees look almost hollow underneath. The deletion of the rocker (not to mention the addition of the external keel) has produced a boat that is probably in large part incapable of achieving the performance characteristics that distinguished the Canadian canoe as a masterpiece of design.

Foiled Again

Another performance feature, which can be totally negated by an unrockered hull with a keel, is the positive hydrodynamic lift to be achieved from paddling with one gunwale lower than the other.

If a lone paddler, paddling either stern first in an empty canoe, or either way in a loaded canoe, trims the boat so the gunwale on his normal paddling side is lower than the other gunwale, a very useful phenomenon occurs.

Bernoulli, a Swiss scientist, formulated his principle at the end of the eighteenth century. It became the basis of all modern developments in flight, sail, and hull design. "In a fluid medium (for example, air, water), acceleration of molecules results in a decrease in pressure."

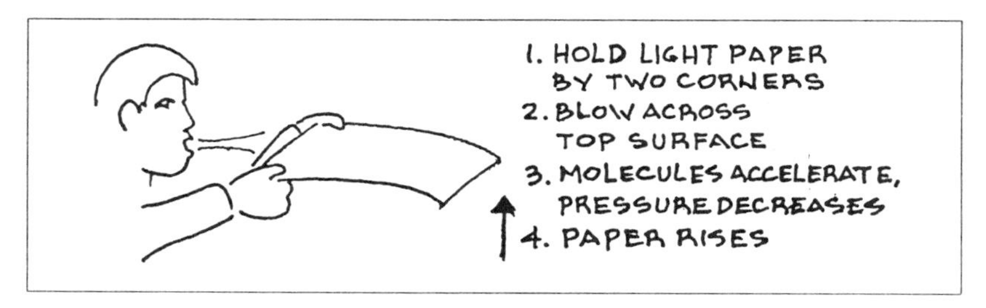

The application of this principle to an airfoil or hydrofoil is that if an unbroken flow can be effected around an asymmetrical foil shape such that the molecules must travel further around one side than the other, those molecules travelling around the longer side will be accelerated, a corresponding decrease in pressure results, and positive lift is realized.

The foil will therefore move through the fluid medium, not only in its forward direction, but also in the direction of the decreased pressure.

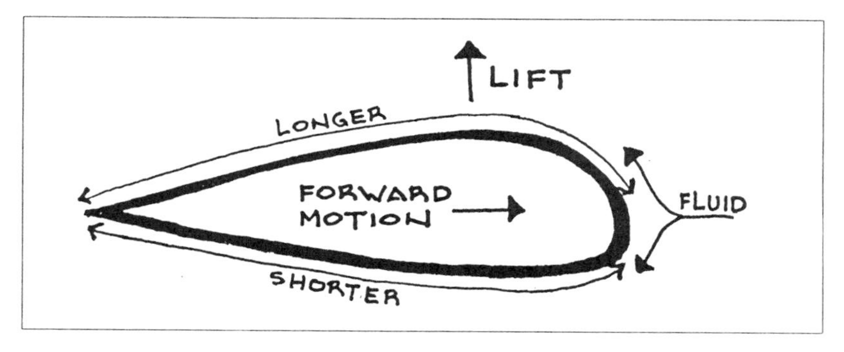

The tilting down of the canoe on the paddling side gunwale lengthens the LWL, and the waterline shape becomes asymmetrical, with the longer side on the paddling side.

The result of this is greater speed as a result of reduced wetted surface (drag) and, most important, positive hydrodynamic lift to the paddling side, thereby in part helping to counteract the tendency of the canoe to turn away from that side as a result of off-center propulsion.

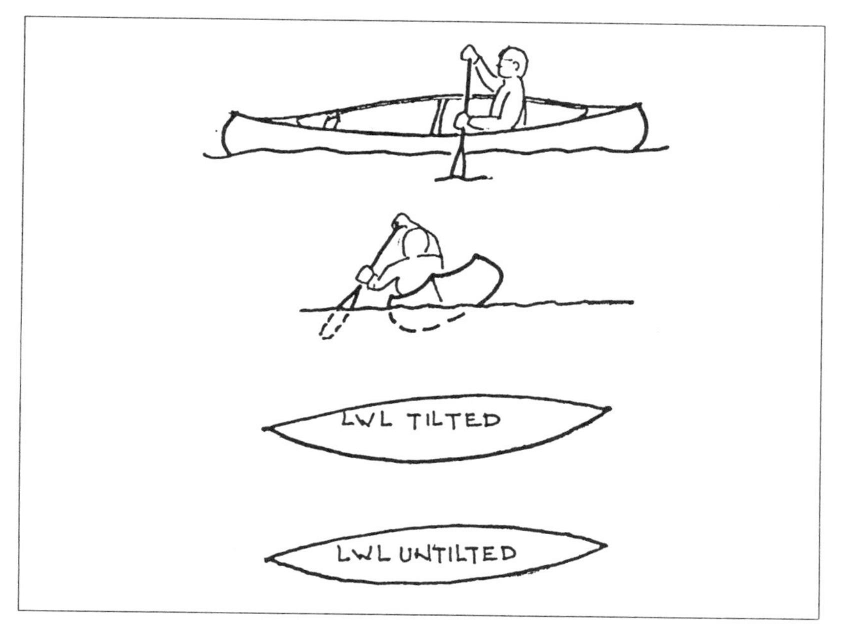

If a lone paddler, moved well forward and paddling stern first, tilts the canoe well over onto the bilge, this phenomenon can be so pronounced as to negate any requirement for directional correction in his paddle stroke.

It must be experienced to be believed!

Keel Or No

Whenever the "experts" mention the subject of keels on canoes, they say that those without keels are more suited to waters where maneuverability is desired, and those with keels are suited to big, open waters, etc., etc.

Where are these "big waters," and what are canoes doing on them anyway? Isn't there a better boat for that purpose?

To set the record straight, no Canadian canoe was ever designed with a keel. Sure, some of the big *canôts de maitre* had keels, both center and bilge, but that was a different game entirely.

The keel on a canoe is strictly a white man's innovation. It was first added because he was disinclined to treat the canoe as did the Indian in order to protect the fragile bark skin, then latterly justified on all sorts of ridiculous grounds like the above.

Hollywood notwithstanding, no birch canoe was ever run up on a beach, or dragged up on shore, or boarded while the stern was still aground. It was carried, carefully, from water to land, and vice versa, boarded only while fully afloat, and laid down, carefully overturned, when not in use.

The white man added the canvas skin, and then tried to beach the canoe, drag it, etc., and found it still wouldn't take that sort of punishment, so he added the keel.

The keel added strength to the hull (and weight), facilitated canvassing and recanvassing, provided an ideal source of leaks, and occasionally helped in scraping over a rock or log in fast water. It also helped compensate for a J-stroker's inability to paddle in a straight line and was the source of considerable turbulence and drag.

Its prime function, however, was to render the boat incapable of the performance characteristics described in previous chapters.

Latterly, the keel has become a feature of most fiberglass and metal canoes because the moulded fold along the chine adds rigidity to the hull and obviates the need for other design features to accomplish this.

I cannot think of one performance increment to be gained from an external keel, and there are certainly decrements, not the least of which is that most hulls with external keels also prove to be unrockered—dead flat!

Eight Canoes

To my knowledge, there have been several different approaches to the construction of the Canadian canoe since the demise of the birch bark model. These are, in approximate chronology, canvas-covered, wood (strip or carvel), moulded plywood, wood plastic, wood glass, aluminum, and fiberglass or plastic.

Each in its time had something to offer, although obviously some did not survive, for whatever reason.

Birch Bark

This was the prototype, with advantages and disadvantages already discussed in some detail.

One point not previously noted was that they were sometimes too light for enjoyable paddling, although this could never be a fault in carrying. A certain mass is desirable in an unloaded canoe in order to maintain momentum, particularly when a hull such as the bark hull produced considerable form resistance. Paddled properly, this disadvantage would be a negligible factor, but a J-stroker probably would find the birch canoe coming to a dead stop between strokes.

Canvas

A damaged bark canoe could be easily repaired with materials immediately at hand in the bush. The canvas, which supplanted bark as the skin on later canoes, was almost as easy to repair. Pitch, made from spruce gum and butter, and a piece of shirttail was usually all that was needed to seal a hole after a patch was whittled out of easily available wood.

Canvas canoes, also ribbed and planked, require thwarts to ensure retention of their shape. The front seat, bolted to the gunwales, could replace a thwart for this purpose, but the rear seat, usually lowered on spacers below the gunwales, could not. Quite often there were one or more intermediate thwarts between the stern seat and the center thwart, and sometimes one was found between the center thwart and bow seat.

Some canoes, constructed solely for "pleasure," had gunwales capped or fully enclosed, but trip canoes invariably left uncovered the rib ends and intervening slots between the inwales and the outwales. This meant that throughout the length of the boat, on both sides, there was ideal provision for lashing all types of cargo.

The wood-canvas canoe was constructed to last much longer than the birch bark-covered ancestor; therefore, certain unattractive features of design that it shared with the bark canoe were more apparent. The bark canoe was usually discarded or rebuilt before these became problems.

As the canoe aged, there was a tendency for the ribs to try to straighten themselves out and return to their natural state. Since the thwarts interfered with this process, the end result quite often was that the flat bottom tended to become rounded over time, and the canoe became narrower with a higher deadrise, slacker bilges, less tumblehome, and resultant instability.

Another problem with canvas canoes was the tendency to gain weight, seasonally and permanently. Any time water got into the bilges for whatever reason, it would wet the canvas and be absorbed into it and any unfinished wood surfaces, resulting in a seasonal gain of as much as ten pounds. Sand and other debris between the planks and canvas also added to weight, as well as contributing to rot and abrasion.

Annually, the requirement to paint and varnish contributed to a permanent and substantial increase in weight.

The appeal of the canvas canoe is legend. Torture boards notwithstanding, the natural feel, the pleasure of a hand-crafted, one-of-a-kind boat, the aesthetics of varnished wood and painted canvas, the silence in the water and out, the natural flotation, etc., are all undeniably attractive features. Labor costs, however, may have relegated the canvas boat to mere memory of things past. As I write this, the word comes that Chestnut has closed, after setting the standards by which all other canoes were judged since almost the turn of the century. Reason given: labour costs, and maybe a lot of people who didn't care about quality.

I am told Chestnut of New Brunswick (and probably Old Town of Maine) made their reputations prior to 1930 by using *Chamaecyparis Thyoides* in the construction of their boats. The local name for this wood was Eastern White Cedar or Atlantic White Cedar. It was harder, more lasting, and tougher than red cedar, but was not common or easy to find. It made a good boat, but the supply eventually ran out, and although the lines of the boats were good, and the construction excellent, that material was no longer available. The lack of that material, and advances in technology, probably contributed to the demise of Chestnut's lead in canoe manufacture.

Carvel Hulls

Strip-planked hulls of varnished and polished cedar or mahogany, with brass bang strips and accessories, were once a common sight. They were seldom designed as work boats, being rather a plaything for beach or cottage. Portability was not a consideration, nor were shape and durability.

These boats have largely disappeared from the scene, and labour costs would preclude their reappearance.

Moulded Plywood

This type of construction resulted from developments in the aircraft industry during World War II. The boats had poor shapes and did not retain these well. Other materials soon supplanted them.

Wood and Plastic

This was essentially a canvas design in which the canvas was replaced with a skin of vinyl or plastic. Any superiority over canvas was negated by problems in repairability and deterioration in sunlight, etc.

Wood and Fiberglass

An early application of "glass" to canoe construction was to replace canvas with fiberglass. This seems to have been a successful venture; however, wood and glass do not weather well together, and who needs ribs in a "glass" boat?

Aluminum

Aluminum boats have the advantage of lightness, durability, freedom from maintenance, and stability in weight. It is a material of minimal aesthetic appeal, alien to the woods, lacking in natural flotation, difficult to repair, and because of rivet heads and dents, may suffer from form resistance over time. It is an ideal boat, if properly moulded, for canoe liveries, outfitters, youth camps and training programs where one can assume a measure of irresponsibility and lack of care.

Fiberglass or plastic (e.g. Kevlar™, Royalex™)

These materials should provide the ultimate in canoe construction. A glass or plastic hull formed from a good mould or plug with wood gunwales and furniture should provide a canoe to satisfy the most demanding standards of any canoeist, traditionalist or progressive.

The material is of proven durability; it is stable, flexible, smooth (inside and out), and with the exceptions of repairability and lack of inherent flotation, appears to have no disadvantages.

In the final analysis, it is not the material, but the shape of the canoe that is critical. A well-shaped hull, which will perform as a canoe should perform, either when paddled or carried, should be the prime consideration in the choice of any canoe.

The Bloody Mary

One of my favorite boats was an Old Town 18-foot canoe. It was a bit heavy to carry, but was well-built, had good lines, and was fast. If a party consisted of three people, it was the answer for fishing, and it had enough room for three passengers. A sixteen-foot boat could accommodate three fishermen, but it was a bit cramped.

Although I never used the twenty-foot boat (square stern) for guiding, it could have been the solution, but it was too heavy to carry and was best propelled by an outboard motor.

The square stern was originally a mapping canoe used by the Department of Mines and Technical Survey. I got it from Jasper, Ontario after they (Mines and Technical Survey) had finished with it. It was somewhat the worse for wear (patched, etc.), but quite seaworthy.

On one occasion, when the whole family used it to watch the airshow from Lake Ontario off Toronto Exhibition Grounds, the Toronto Harbour Police accosted us, but couldn't find anything wrong. We had life jackets for each person aboard, paddles for all, running lights, a bailer, and ample rope, and the whole thing was pushed by a 7½-horsepower motor (registration was mandatory if the motor was over 10 h.p.). They finally gave up looking for something wrong and went away shaking their heads. They had never run into anything like that before.

It was a big boat, had plenty of room, and was very stable. Had it not been a square stern, it probably would have measured 25 feet.

On one occasion, there were twenty-plus adults aboard, with lawn chairs and people walking around, but with no problems.

What had happened was that we started out with only two people aboard and a gallon of Bloody Marys, and we dock-hopped. At each dock, someone joined the party. After several docks, the Bloody Marys ran out, so we had to go back for more. But the passenger list kept increasing.

It was a good party, even though we had to go back to replenish the jug several times. That happened for several years.

When I left that part of the world to go West, I was informed I could go, but the boat would stay on the lake to fulfill the function of the "Bloody Mary boat." I was to get one share, and the other shares would be paid for by several interested parties. That arrangement suited me, so the deal was consummated. The boat, motor, and trailer are still there, even after all these years.

2

Paddling

Reminiscences

My first recollection of boating was of being in a canoe, and throughout my early years, the canvas canoe and Peterborough clinker-built rowing skiff were the only boats I knew.

Among other things during this period, I learned respect for the instability of the canoe. I also learned to kneel while paddling, never to let the fragile canvas touch shore or bottom, never to allow the paddle to touch the gunwale while paddling, and never to drip water into the hull. I learned to haul the canoe out of the water over my thigh and leave it overturned while not in use, and to do annual maintenance on boat and paddles with paint and varnish. I didn't learn to carry, or to paddle particularly well.

Around the age of twelve, I acquired my first canoe. For years, I had been aware of a derelict with a stove-in bow underneath the verandah of my paternal grandfather's cottage. Now, across the road from my maternal grandfa-

ther's farmhouse, lived a carpenter/builder. One evening, sitting on the front stoop, he mentioned a canoe for sale.

It seems he had taken the derelict as partial payment for some work he had done on the cottage, had repaired it, and now wished to realize his money. The price was ten dollars, so I bought it.

As canoes go, it was a monstrosity. Originally a cedar-strip (carvel) hull, of dubious shape, it had subsequently been canvassed, then half-canvassed again. There may have been seats in it once, but now there were only thwarts, and heavy ones at that. It weighed about 100 pounds (for a 16-foot hull), and for a twelve year old might as well have weighed 500 pounds. It was, however, a boat, and above all, *my* boat.

Even at that age, I was an avid reader of the only two existent outdoor magazines: *Outdoor Life* and *Field and Stream.* My uncle, a pharmacist, had a large magazine counter. When an issue of a periodical expired, he removed the cover to exchange for the next issue and discarded the magazine. It didn't matter to me that it was a month out of date.

It was in one of these magazines that I came across a short anecdote that suggested to me that there was more to the art of paddling than I had been aware of.

As I recollect, the anecdote went something like this:

> An American writer, who claimed to be young, fit, athletic, and an experienced canoeist, was visiting James Bay. One day he had occasion to paddle from Moosenee to Moose Factory across the Moose River.
>
> As he set out against a fairly strong headwind in a new, modern, canvas canoe, an old Indian woman departed simultaneously, presumably for the same destination. She appeared to be in her late sixties or seventies, under 100 pounds in weight, and paddling an old bark canoe, badly misshapen, with several broken ribs.
>
> His initial reaction was to "show her how a canoe should be paddled," but he soon had cause to reassess the situation. In spite of every effort he could make, to the point of approaching total exhaustion at the trip's end, he found that not only could he not win this "race," he could not even keep up with her, and fell farther and farther behind.
>
> As a result of this experience, he began to examine the strange, awkward paddling style of the local Crees in a more positive fashion, and he tried to describe it in the article.
>
> He noted that they used extremely long paddles, with long, slim blades. They paddled with an effortless twisting motion of the torso, with the upper arm almost straight, and the lower arm barely moving from the side. The upper hand seemed to describe small, continuous circles or ovals above the head, and the strokes were extremely short and fast, approaching 50 per minute, with no pause or appar-

ent effort to steer the canoe, yet the course never varied or veered, except as the paddler desired.

Propulsion

In the same way that primitive man evolved unique solutions in his design of boats, his propulsion techniques also varied widely in different parts of the world. One area of commonality was apparent, however. Whenever possible, if his primary source of energy was manpower, he utilized, to the greatest extent possible, the musculature of his legs and torso.

An unforgettable sight is the Oriental fisherman, propelling a very substantial cabin boat, which houses his whole family, at an incredible speed with a single twenty-foot *yuloh*, or sculling oar. He walks this back and forth on his after deck, utilizing the full potential of his legs and body strength as he pushes and pulls.

The conventional rowing technique popular in Europe and much of the world deliberately sacrifices forward visibility for the capability of using the power of the legs and torso. Anyone who has tried rowing a boat facing forward is immediately aware of the diminution of power compared to rowing with one's back to the bow.

Paddling, by comparison, is a very inefficient method of propulsion. It is appropriate, however, if conditions render other methods unacceptable. The lone hunter (or hunted) does not want his back to his destination. Neither does the white-water paddler, nor the Eskimo facing large breakers or turbulent water. A double paddle is more appropriate for their purpose, facilitating control and the uprighting of a craft overturned, accidentally or intentionally. A narrow hull, necessitating an outrigger, precludes the use of oars or a double paddle, as do constricted, convoluted, or weed-choked waterways.

In situations where a single-bladed paddle was appropriate, paddling invariably incorporated methods that, to whatever extent possible, maximized the use of the large muscles of the body and minimized the involvement of the relatively weaker arm muscles, particularly if paddling was to be done for protracted periods of time.

The arm muscles could always be brought into play in situations where more speed or extra power was needed.

Paddling Techniques

Suppose you were the driver of an automobile with an automatic transmission and weak shocks, and you proceeded in the following manner:

> With one foot on the gas and the other on the brake you applied them alternately, and each time you pressed the gas you turned the wheel to the right, and each time you pressed the brake you turned the wheel to the left.

Apart from the fact that no examiner would ever license you, an observer would see the following:

> A vehicle accelerating and decelerating down the road, body rising and falling as the springs and weak shocks are overworked, and all the time weaving like a drunken sailor.

Well, the foregoing describes precisely the result of that anathema of paddling technique, the J-stroke.

The J-stroke is a technique whereby, after the propulsion stroke, a correction is applied for the turning off-course of the canoe as a result of the off-centre propulsion. The arms reach well forward, the blade is inserted into the water to propel the canoe forward, then the upper wrist is turned 90 degrees to make the paddle a steering oar (blade up and down), and the correction is applied. The paddle blade moves in a pattern like the letter "J."

Strangely, most of the pundits, after describing something called the basic stroke, then go on to advocate the use of the J-stroke, dismissing a mysterious technique they variously describe as the "guide's stroke," "Indian stroke," or "Canadian stroke," as something beyond the capability of any normal paddler.

It is hoped that they don't apply the same reasoning to the operation of their automobiles!

Earlier, I made reference to an anecdote that suggested to me at an early age that something better than the J-stroke existed. Simply stated, the technique incorporates the following:

— Use of the back and torso muscles rather than the arms.
— Except in emergency situations, the paddler attempts specifically not to "pull water," or exert effort.
— Speed, rather than power, is the secret of the stroke, not unlike the gear changes of an automobile, wherein once momentum is achieved through the use of power gears, it is maintained through the use of speed and not power.
— All control of direction and correction for the turning moment resultant from paddling on one side is effected during (not after) the power stroke.

THE STROKE: (All descriptions are those of a right-handed paddler, that is, paddling on the left side of the canoe)

First, tie the left elbow to your belt at the left side with four inches or less of cord in between. Grasp the paddle with the left hand at the throat, the top of the blade just below where the round shaft begins to broaden and flatten into the blade (Fig. 1). Extend the left forearm outside,

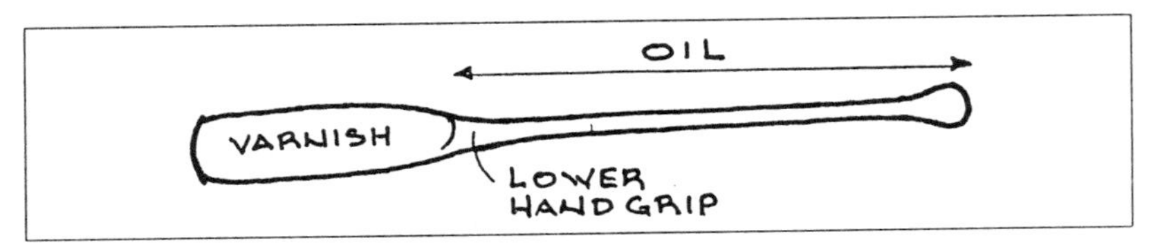

Figure 1

above and roughly parallel to the gunwale. The wrist should be bent slightly down, the flat of the blade facing up and down, and the whole paddle at right angles to the canoe gunwales, but slanting down so that the tip of the blade is just clear of the water and the butt end high above the right shoulder (Fig. 2).

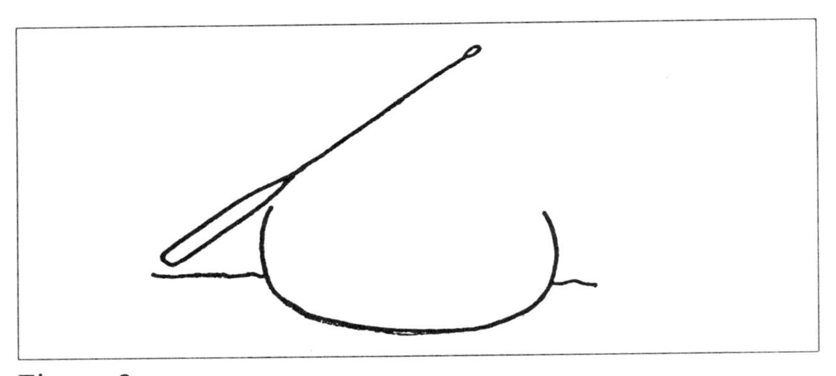
Figure 2

Now reach up and grasp the butt with the right hand above the head, with the right elbow locked but not rigidly straight, and the wrist bent slightly down.

Cock both wrists up. This rotates the paddle 90 degrees, and now the blade is edges up and down (Fig. 3). At the same time, commence to rotate the torso left (anti-clockwise), which swings the right arm to the left, and commence to lower the left forearm. This drops the blade into the water and the paddle is now approaching vertical, with the blade immersed (Fig. 4).

Continue to rotate the torso, keeping the right arm rigid

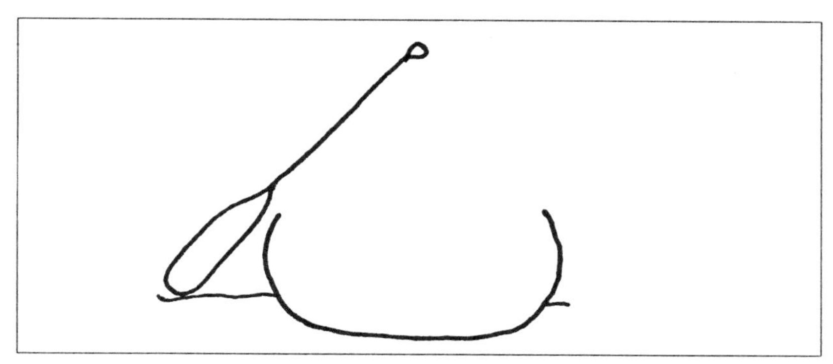

Figure 3

(do not flex), and simultaneously lower the left forearm and hand, but do not pull with the left hand. Because the left elbow is tied to the waist, the left forearm and hand can function only as an articulated rowlock.

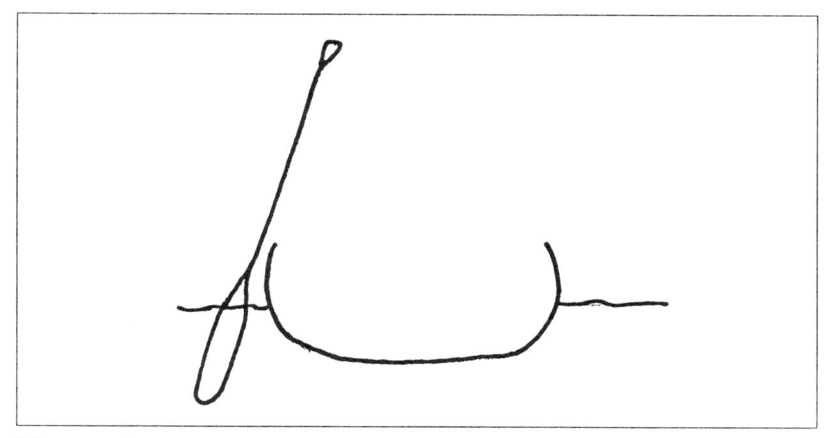

Figure 4

When the short power stroke has reached the limit imposed by the immobilized left elbow, rigid right arm, and limited ability of the torso to rotate, then untwist the torso, simultaneously turning both wrists so that the flat of the blade now is feathered, or facing up (and is actually angled slightly up on the forward edge), and moving forward through the water to surface finally in the position at which the next stroke commences.

It should be noted that the relaxed elbow of the left arm allows the forearm to swing up and down to facilitate the entry and exit of the blade in the water, while the right hand describes continuous circles or small ovals in a horizontal plane distinctly inclined to the right.

It cannot be emphasized too strongly that one of the requirements of this technique is that once momentum has been attained, the paddler should consciously try not to "pull water." On several occasions, I have instructed bow paddlers to "go through the motions only" and just pretend they are paddling. Without their knowledge, I have then simply used my stern paddle as a rudder and watched their amazement when they discovered that the not inconsiderable speed at which we were travelling was attributable solely to their attempt at "faking."

Because the strokes are very short, they can be very fast: 40 to 50 strokes per minute. This would be an impossible pace to maintain for any length of time if any arm muscles were involved, or if the paddler reached and pulled, or if correction for direction were to be applied after the power stroke. If, however, only the large muscles of the torso are worked, and the arms are only used to attach the paddle to these muscles, and if no conscious effort is made, one can maintain this stroke effortlessly for hours on end.

Directional Control

The prime concern here is to counteract the turning moment resultant from applying the propellant force off-center as a result of paddling on one side of the canoe only. If the paddler is conceptualized as the center of a source of energy, and he applies the propellant force on a chord of an arc surrounding him, then Newton's First Law (which states that for every action there is an equal and opposite reaction) will cause his body to rotate in the opposite direction from that of the force he applies to the paddle. Since he is (presumably) in some manner attached to the hull, this turning moment will also be imparted to the hull and translated into a tendency to turn away from the side on which the paddling is being done.

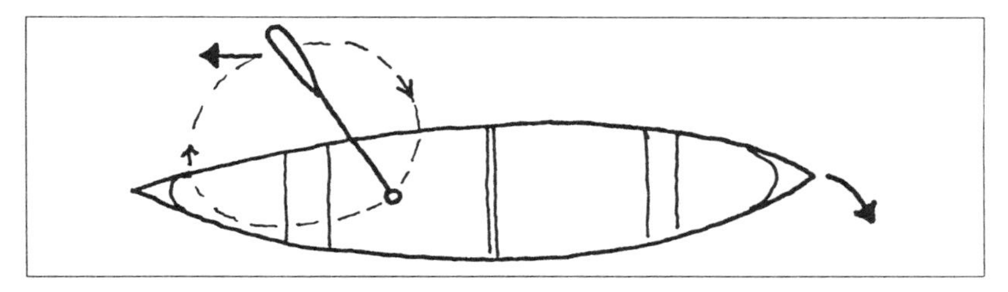

Now, to counteract this phenomenon simply requires a re-application of Newton's Law.

If you sit in a canoe (afloat) and grasp the piling of a dock (which is anchored solidly to the bottom) and try to rotate it, it will not rotate, but you and the canoe will rotate in the opposite direction to that which you tried to impart to the piling.

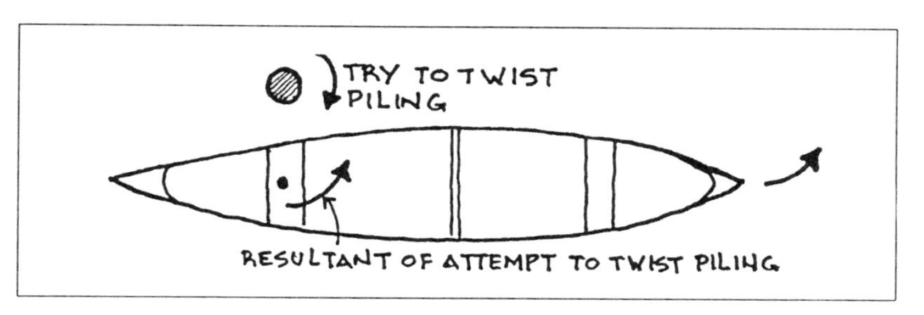

A paddle, inserted more or less vertically in the water, is not solidly anchored as was the piling; nevertheless, the blade can provide considerable resistance to a rotating moment, thereby translating an opposite rotation to the paddler's body (and canoe). This is precisely what is done during the power stroke, to counteract the tendency of the canoe to turn off course.

As the power stroke is applied, the paddle is rotated around its vertical axis in a clockwise direction, so that the inner edge of the blade is "throwing" more water than the outer edge.

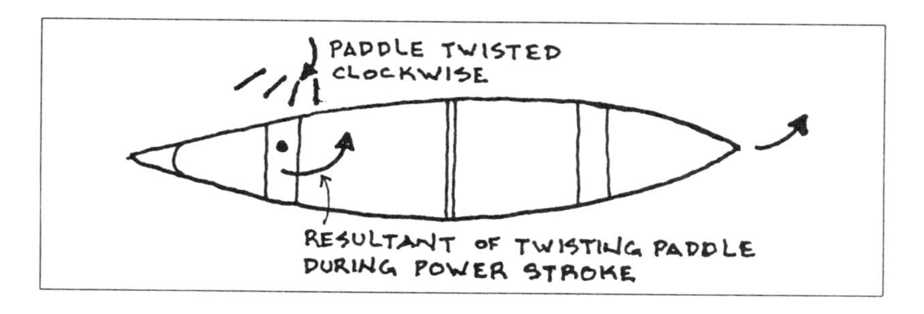

The "equal and opposite" effect of this is to apply a counter-clockwise turning moment to the paddler (and canoe) that can cancel out the clockwise turning momentum resultant from off-center paddling. The end result, when it is properly applied, is that the canoe moves through the water in a dead straight line.

This turning or rotation of the paddle is accomplished primarily by the right hand on the butt of the paddle, but if the left hand is grasping the paddle on the flattened neck of the blade, the fingers of the left hand can also influence this turning moment.

The need for this control by the stern paddler varies with load and conditions. Less correction is required if a bow paddler is paddling on the opposite side, or if there is a wind coming from the starboard side, or if there is lift resulting from paddling gunwales down, etc. The important point to note is that all corrective action must be completed by the end of a very short power stroke, and without in any way interfering with the rhythm or pace of paddling.

Now the automobile proceeds smoothly down the road, neither accelerating nor decelerating, rising nor falling, and in a straight line.

And now your paddle sings, and oh, what a song!

Paddles

It must be obvious by now that the usual off-the-rack paddles available at marinas, outfitters, and sporting goods stores are going to be unsatisfactory, if for no other reason than they will be too short.

The paddle needed to utilize the foregoing technique must be close to the paddler's height. It should, at least, reach his nose and preferably be forehead height or longer. About one-third of its length should be blade, two-thirds shaft. With that length of blade, it becomes necessary that the blade be narrow, no wider than 4 inches, because only a certain area of blade is controllable. Beyond that, extra area is an unproductive nuisance, so the longer the blade, the narrower it must be.

The length of shaft is needed to allow the comfortable use of the arms as described, and in terms of a Class I lever, the longer the shaft, the better.

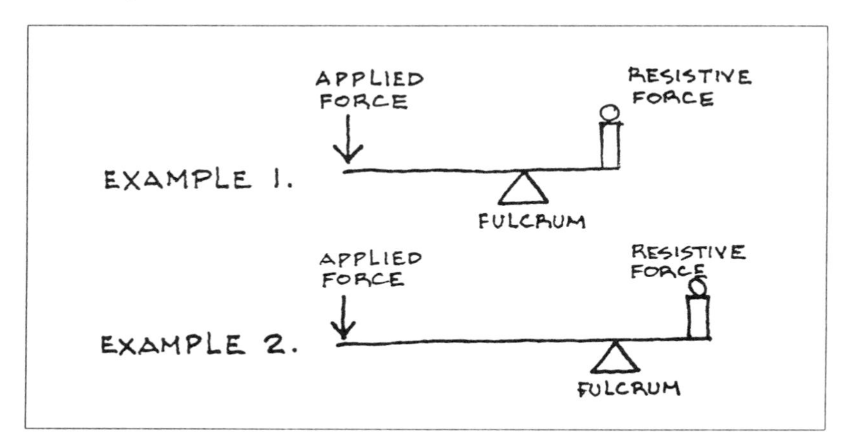

Obviously the pry obtained by Example 2 is much more efficient than Example 1 for the same amount of applied force because of the longer lever. If one envisages the left hand as the fulcrum, blade against the water as resistive force, and the right hand on the butt of the paddle as force applied, the logic is inescapable.

One might tolerate a long shaft with a short, wide blade; however, surface water is swept around more easily than deep water, and our objective is to approximate as closely as possible a situation where the paddle is anchored firmly in the water.

"Okay," you ask, "If you're so smart, why ain't you rich? How come all the paddles available are short-shafted and broad-bladed?"

I suspect that one reason is that pattern lathes (machines that duplicate a model or pattern) are designed for furniture-making and other purposes that do not necessitate a bed length of 64 inches to 74 inches. They probably are only capable of a maximum of 60 inches.

Most paddles are designed to be sold to motorboat owners, who are required, by law, to carry two paddles, or one paddle, one bucket, and 50 feet of string, etc.

Racing paddlers, who paddle over short distances, utilizing a maximum expenditure of energy, prefer short, broad paddles and, therefore, to some extent, influence design standards.

Anyone who is satisfied to use the J-stroke or similar techniques is likely to be satisfied with any shape of oar; what difference could it make?

So how does one acquire a satisfactory paddle? Unless you're lucky, either custom-made, or do-it-yourself.

One advantage of a long paddle is that there are not infrequent occasions when the best method of propulsion in narrow, shallow waterways is poling. If this is not to be a protracted session of poling, the canoeist often does not want to take time out to cut (and shoe) a pole, so if his paddle is long enough, he makes do with it as a temporary pole.

This does not work too well if the paddle is of softwood because the end of the blade soon chips or splits. Otherwise, certain softwoods make satisfactory paddles. It takes more bulk of softwood, however, to achieve the same strength as a finer hardwood blade.

There are two favorite woods for paddle-making: rock maple and black cherry. Both are close-grained, flexible, and strong, and take a high finish. Possibly some of the new laminated techniques could produce a satisfactory paddle. I have never seen anything shaped like a paddle produced in this fashion, but that may simply be a function of design, rather than a limitation of the material.

The shape of the blade and butt are matters of personal preference. The only requirements are that the paddle balance reasonably well where the lower hand grips it, that the shape of the butt facilitate control by the right (upper) hand, and that the blade be well-varnished where it is submerged in use, with the balance (throat to butt) well-oiled where the hands come in contact with it.

A paddle blank, band-sawed from a clear 1¼-inch board can be completely shaped and finished with nothing more exotic than a half-round rasp, a half-round crosscut file, several grades of sandpaper, varnish, and linseed oil. If checks (splits) occur during or after construction in the blade or butt ends, run a thin sawblade into and past the check, fill with epoxy cement, and sand smooth when dry. One used to repair checks in the blade by drilling small holes and lacing the check with snare wire, but I have repairs of over twenty-five years vintage done with epoxy cement, and they are still sound.

Different Strokes

Obviously, there are circumstances under which the foregoing techniques will not provide the immediate and drastic change of direction required. The following are some strokes, which used singly or in combination, by one or more paddlers, will usually suffice to provide the directional control needed for any situation.

Sweep

This technique can be envisaged as using the paddle as one would use the oar on a rowboat. With the paddle blade extended well out from the side of the canoe in an almost horizontal position, the blade is immersed shallowly to provide a turning moment to the hull.

A combination of a forward sweep on one side, followed by a reverse sweep on the other, has the same effect as using the two oars on a rowboat in opposition; that is, the craft can be rotated 180 degrees in its own length.

Various effects can be obtained by bow and stern paddlers combining sweep strokes.

A variation of the sweep stroke, called "paddling wide," is used by a stern paddler when paddling against a crosswind coming from the off side (the other side from the one on which he is paddling).

Draw

A paddle inserted vertically in the water at some distance from the canoe with the flat of the blade parallel to the gunwale and drawn directly toward the canoe will cause the canoe to move sideways toward the paddle. If the movement is repeated by feathering the paddle at the end of each draw and returning to the original position, a steady sideways pull may be imparted to the hull.

Pry

This is the opposite to the draw. The blade is inserted at an angle under the hull, the shaft is pried on the gunwale, and the paddle is feathered to return to the original position.

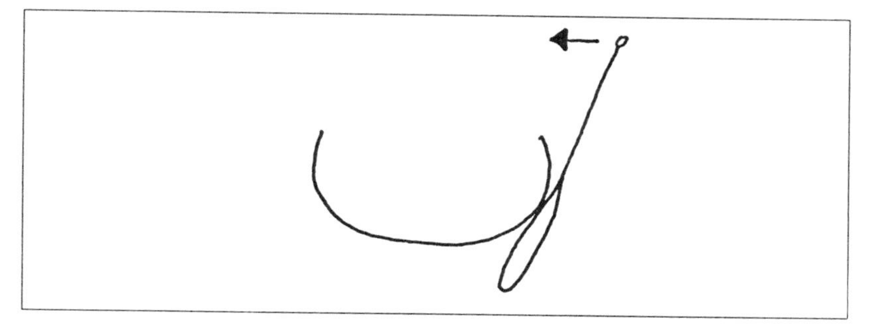

This stroke will move the hull sideways away from the side on which the paddle is being used.

Jam

This stroke is used to apply the brakes or stop forward motion. The paddle is inserted in the water, the blade at right angles to the gunwale, and the shaft vertical. To use it, one must hold on to the gunwale and paddle simultaneously with the lower hand. It must be used with caution because it can easily capsize the canoe and is best used by bow and stern paddlers simultaneously.

Backwater

If the jam stroke has stopped the canoe's motion and there is a need to reverse further, backwater, the reverse of the basic forward stroke, is used; again, preferably by both bow and stern in unison.

Bow Rudder

The bow paddler may impart a violent change in direction by use of the sweep, draw, or pry, particularly if coordinated with an appropriate complementary action from the stern. Another stroke is the bow rudder, which is not dissimilar to the jam stroke except the blade is angled in the direction desired for the canoe to turn, and the paddle is inserted into the water as far ahead as can be managed easily by the paddler. This stroke also requires a firm grip by the lower hand on the shaft and gunwale.

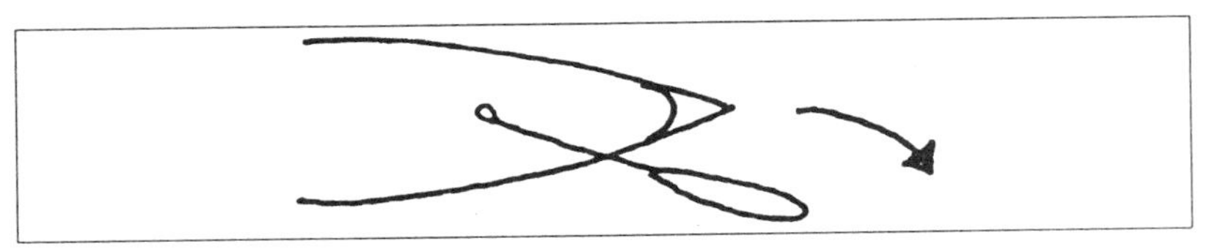

Stern Rudder

This involves the stern paddler utilizing his paddle as a steering oar only, trailing it aft as a rudder and providing no propulsion.

Crossbow Rudder

A technique that produces an immediate and substantial change in direction, the crossbow rudder requires a long paddle. The bowman places the blade across the stem of the canoe so that part of the blade is inserted in the water on the opposite side at an angle of 30 - 45 degrees.

It must be done without shifting the grip on the paddle as it is a "panic stations" technique. This requires that the arms be crossed to apply it from the same side as that on which the bowman is paddling, or the blade be lifted over the bow to apply it from the other side.

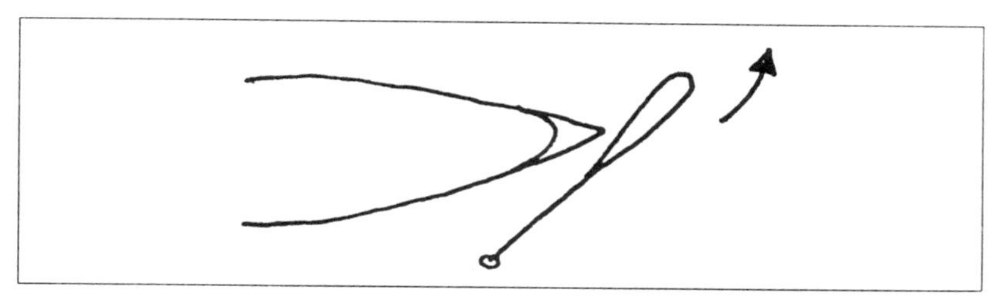

Sculling

A technique used in either a push or pull mode for continuous sideways motion of the hull, the flat of the blade is positioned parallel to the gunwale with the shaft almost vertical. The paddle is moved in short arcs back and forth through the water, the leading edge angled away from the boat for a draw effect to move the hull toward it, or angled toward the boat to provide a pry effect. The paddle is not feathered for a recovery stroke; rather, the leading edge changes depending on direction and is constantly angled appropriately for the direction in which the paddle is moving through the water.

3

Transporting Canoes

Besides Paddling

When a canoe is not to be paddled, there are several alternative means of moving it on the water:

Sail

Equipped with leeboards hinged on either end of a bracket clamped across the gunwales amidships and a small lateen or lugs'l, the canoe has a reasonable capability upwind and excellent downwind performance.

Power

Small gas or electric outboards up to three horsepower will propel a canoe at hull speed. The "V" stern power canoe in lengths over 18 or 19 feet permits the motor to drive from the centerline, and the canoe retains all its paddling characteristics. Under 18 feet, the motor on the stern transom is too inaccessible to the operator for refuelling, starting, steering, etc., and places too much weight aft.

A motor clamped onto a bracket, which in turn is clamped across the gunwales within the reach of the operator, has the advantage of ease in handling and better fore and aft weight distribution, but the disadvantage of off-center propulsion and weight.

Rowing

A light set of sculls, with rowlocks on the gunwales and the rower seated down in the hull on a cushion or two, is one of the most efficient ways of propelling a canoe. Because of the relatively narrow beam, it is necessary that the butt ends of the oars overlap substantially.

Until you have seen a canoe under two sets of light oars, you would not believe the speed to be achieved! Why more people who operate canoes in relatively open water, and who obviously can't paddle, do not try oars, I'll never understand.

Poling

Under certain conditions of depth and current, a canoe will make better progress when poled rather than paddled.

Poles are cut as needed, approximately 1½ inches in diameter and up to canoe length. Sometimes paddlers carry a steel shoe to be affixed to the pole with a nail or set screw.

A right-handed paddler would stand forward of the stern seat, slightly inclined to the left, holding the pole with the right hand as high as depth of water permits and the left hand two feet lower. The pole is thrust into the bottom, keeping it about 6 inches from the gunwale.

As the canoe is pushed forward, work your hands up the pole like climbing a rope. Steering is done by pushing outward or pulling inward with the upper hand and against the lower hand as a fulcrum, much as one might do with a paddle.

Stern poling may be combined with a bowman paddling or poling to provide propulsion against a current, or a braking effect on a downstream run.

Tracking

In water too fast for paddling and too deep for poling, a canoe may be tracked upstream from shore by two lines affixed bow and stern to provide both propulsion and steering. The trick is to keep the bow slightly out in current at all times, not so much as to lose control, but enough to keep the current from driving the boat ashore.

Towing

The only way to tow a canoe behind a power boat, empty or loaded, is with a bridle. Attach the bridle around the canoe from roughly the location of the bow seat, with the towing lead off the bridle dead center and coming from under the keel line.

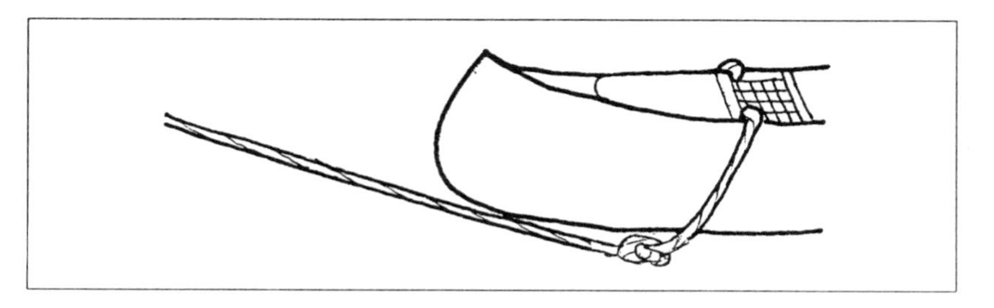

On A Canoe

Provided there is only the lightest of breezes, one paddler can transport one or two other canoes atop his canoe quite comfortably. To try to tow when paddling is folly, but another canoe, right side up and balanced across the gunwales is quite a practical proposition.

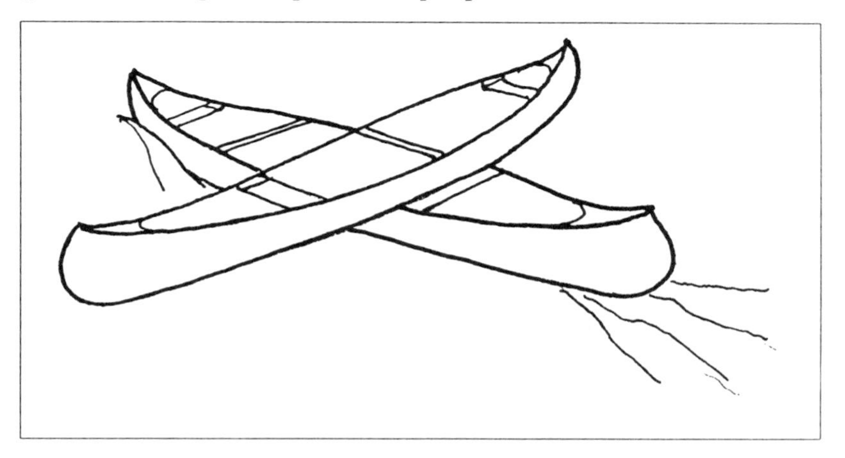

Car-Top Transportation

Before the advent of roof racks, various ingenious devices were employed to transport canoes on top of cars. Even after the suction cup type of roof carrier became popular, the canoe still had to have bow and stern lines lashed to the front and rear bumper to ensure safety, and these lines inevitably interfered with access to the engine and luggage compartments.

It seemed that no sooner was the canoe securely lashed down the radiator boiled over, or someone wanted the sandwich basket and lemonade jug out of the trunk.

The advent of bolted or clamped on racks changed all that, but there is still good cause for ensuring that a canoe, once on top of a vehicle, stays there. I can't imagine anything worse than driving down the highway at 60 mph to suddenly find that the vehicle in front is about to deposit its canoe through your windshield.

I have seen canoes held on with old bicycle inner tubes, binder twine, bungy straps, and the idiot web straps and friction buckles sold with some types of roof racks. None of these have I seen from behind at highway speeds. I choose to be elsewhere.

If you are satisfied that your car-top roof racks bolt or clamp securely, proceed as follows:

- Place the canoe on them, gunwales down and reasonably well-centered.
- Use good rope! Someone's life may depend on it, and check it frequently for wear. Braided or twist dacron or nylon, 5/16 inch or larger is quite adequate. Poly and plastics are lacking in tensile strength, deteriorate in sunlight, are hard to handle, and are too slippery to knot well.
- With the canoe loaded, tie a length of rope securely to the roof rack beside the gunwale on one side. Toss the rope over the canoe, and go around to the other side.
- Tie a bight (loop, eye) in the rope about one foot above the roof rack. Take the end of the rope under the bar of the rack and back up through the bight.
- Now with all your strength pull down on the end of the rope, as though the bight was a pulley. Make the canoe groan. Holding the tension, tie a half hitch at the bight and take the end around the bar of the rack

again. Tie securely, or windlass the two strands together to obtain even more tension, then tie.

- Repeat with the other rack, and there is no way (unless your knots are defective) that the canoe will ever move, because it is secured fore and aft of its greatest beam, and locked solidly to the roof racks

Portaging

Portability is the single outstanding characteristic of the Canadian canoe that differentiates it from all other craft and that uniquely suits it for wilderness travel. As its shape permits the navigation of narrow, tortuous, weed-choked waterways, so it is conducive to being carried through the thick brush of an uncleared portage. Many other boats are light enough to be carried, but their wide beam or blunt ends render carrying through brush-choked trails an exercise in futility.

In the business of portability, the white man has again attempted to improve on the intent of the original designers with results that are patently counter-productive. For some years, he carried an extra paddle for the express purpose of using its blade as one of a pair to carry on. Today we have an abomination in the shape of a yoke replacing the centre thwart.

The first requirement for portability is, of course, that the boat be light enough to carry comfortably. Somewhere between 60 and 85 pounds, depending on length, is acceptable, particularly if a pack is also to be carried. The lighter the better, provided structural safety is not compromised.

Next, there is balance. A canoe should balance reasonably well at the center thwart. With the wrists crossed, pick the canoe up by the gunwale, one hand on either side of and up against the center thwart. If neither bow nor stern feels heavier, there is reasonable balance. Small differences may be easily adjusted.

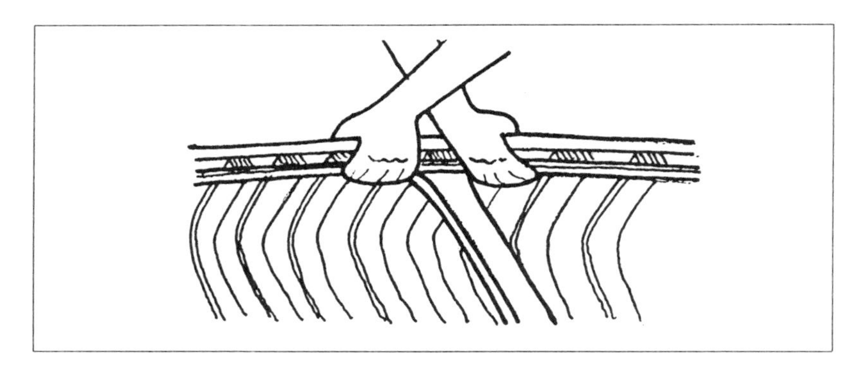

Now the Indians did not have the benefit of Newton's Law of Gravity, but they understood that a weight could be carried with less effort if supported by a column of bone, rather than bringing extraneous muscles into play. A load carried on the arms or shoulders necessitated the involvement of those muscles before the bone column of the spine, pelvis, legs could transmit the downward thrust of the weight to the ground.

On the other hand, a weight carried on top of the head, as done by so many primitive peoples around the world, only involved a direct downward thrust through the bony skeletal column. So the Indians either carried on top of the head (often using a hat padded with straw), or with a tumpline on top of the head, or with the thwart resting on the spine at shoulder level, or any combination of these.

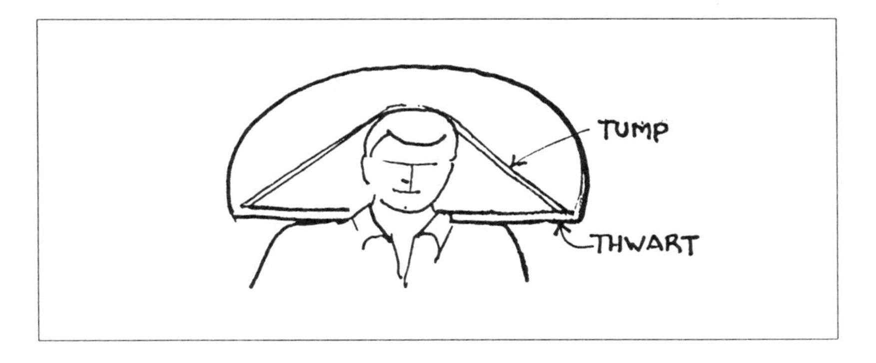

No paddles, no yokes, and no arm or shoulder involvement. Besides, if one has to carry a pack as well, there is not much choice except to carry the pack on shoulder straps, so why double-burden the shoulders?

In certain situations, it is also critical that a canoe can be picked up and carried in a certain direction. What if the yoke is facing the other way? What if there isn't time to tie the paddles in? What if you lose one paddle?

Imagine a situation where you suddenly find yourself in a deep canyon with white water that is impassable. By sheer luck you find a narrow ledge and get ashore holding your canoe. The ledge leads you up to safety in one direction only, but your yoke is facing the other direction, and there is no room to turn around. If you try to swing the canoe out to turn it around, the force of the current is quite likely to sweep it out of your grasp and leave you stranded. What do you do?

Learn to carry the way it was designed to be carried!

The Lift and the Carry

First, take off your heavy wool shirt, hold it by both cuffs, arms outstretched, and flip it a few times so that the body of the shirt rolls up on itself. Then tie the sleeves around your neck with a half hitch, so that the rolled up body makes a pad behind your neck.

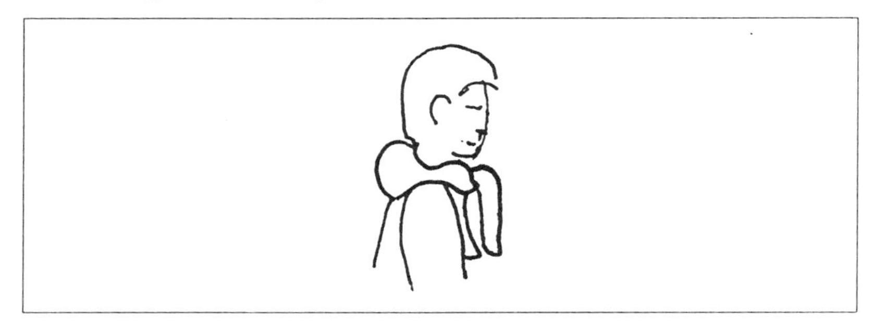

Now standing amidships, face the canoe. Depending whether you wish to march off to your right or left, nominate the appropriate hand (right or left) to reach across and grasp the center thwart where it joins the far gunwale. As you stoop to do so, the other arm simultaneously reaches under the canoe, as though you were trying to touch the keel line.

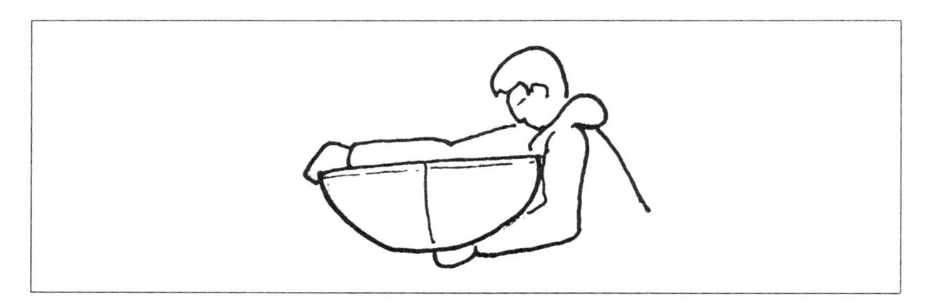

Pulling the thwart toward you and lifting on your other forearm, lift the canoe off the ground or out of the water with the center thwart vertical, and when the body has straightened up, the centerline (keel line) is at shoulder level.

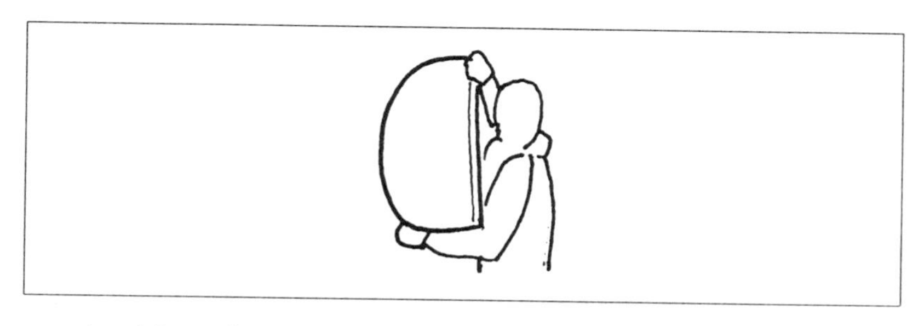

At this point, the whole body does a 90-degree pivot, and simultaneously, the hand on the thwart pulls the thwart over the head and back of it, so that the upturned canoe is on top of the head and the thwart is centered on the pad behind the neck.

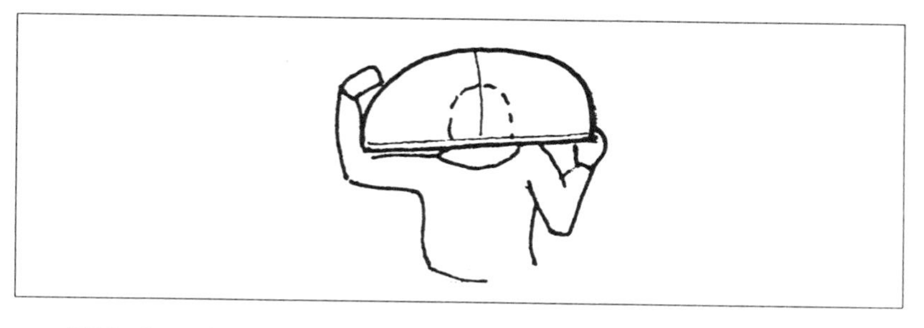

This hand now reaches forward to grasp the gunwale as far forward as possible on that side, and the other arm around the outside of the hull is lowered.

The upraised shoulder of the hand grasping the gunwale helps to keep the thwart on the neck pad, and the other hand is free to swing, carry the paddle, swat mosquitoes, scratch, pick flowers, or just rest. Hands can be changed as frequently as cramped muscles dictate.

If you can predict the direction in which you will carry, or have a particularly long carry to make, it pays to balance the canoe so that it is slightly down to the rear, in such a way that the arm and hand on the gunwale will apply only enough weight to pull the front down far enough to still allow good visibility forward.

A further refinement is to use a tumpline. If tied to both gunwales about 1½ to 2 inches ahead of the center thwart and adjusted to an appropriate length, when over the top of the head, a downward pull on the front of the canoe will shift the weight from the thwart to the tump.

Personal preference is the rule, but never to the extent that the canoe cannot be picked up and carried in any situation, from any position, and in any direction.

For example, it used to be common practice to remove the center thwart, saw or chisel off ¼ inch from one end and replace it to leave a slot in which the axe blade could be wedged. The axe was then lashed under the gunwale, and by adjusting the axe head back and forth or lashing the axe helve bow or stern first, the balance of the canoe could be adjusted to suit.

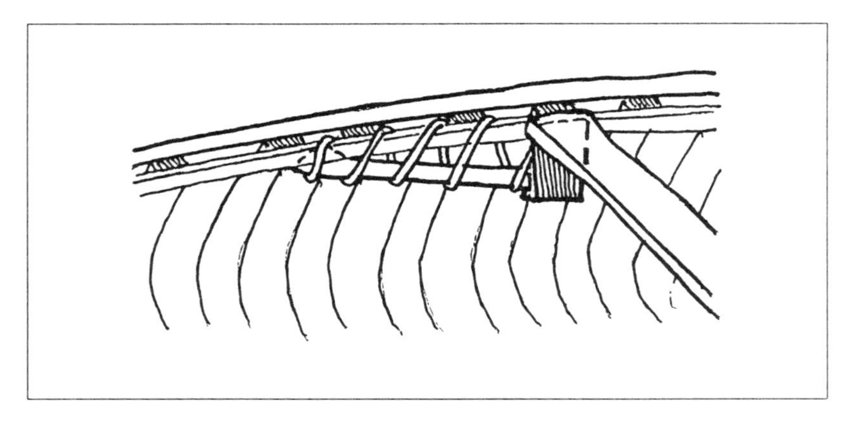

This procedure had an additional benefit in that a good axe was too long to fit in a pack, and in any case was safer and more likely to be available or retrievable in case of accident or emergency.

In situations where the portage direction was predictable, I used to prefer to counterbalance the stern heavily enough so that, with my hand on the gunwale and my paddle pushed up into the bow, the rear was still down far enough to permit good forward visibility.

Prior to picking up the canoe, I would go down the trail a few feet and set the paddle upright in a bush, or lean it against a tree. As I passed it with the canoe on top, I would pick it up with the free hand and push it up into the front of the canoe, to be held in place by the hand grasping the gunwale.

4

Some Random Thoughts

To Sit Or Not To Sit

"And there it is, straight from Hollywood! The intrepid mountain man and his faithful Indian ally, J-stroking their bark canoe through the rapids, perched high on the canoe seats, knees under their chins."

One of the most conclusive manifestations of ignorance about canoes and canoeing in general is the prevalence of the practice of sitting up on canoe seats, especially by bow paddlers.

"So what?" you ask, "If seats are there, are they not meant to be sat upon?"

No, they are not, and I will attempt to explain why.

One of the criteria for safety afloat in any boat is to keep the center of gravity (C of G) as low as possible. A canoe, without cargo or ballast, floats very high in the water, and is very unstable as a result. It therefore behooves the canoeist to ensure that, as he adds ballast, he places it as low as possible. If the ballast is only his body weight, he should ensure that it (his body) is placed as low as possible, taking cognizance of his need to manipulate the paddle.

Furthermore, because of the inherent instability of the craft and his need to control its direction, there is also a requirement that in some fashion he is "locked in" to the craft so that both paddler and canoe function as a single unit.

This certainly cannot be effected if he is perched up on a seat with his knees up in the air.

Now, a lone paddler can, to some extent, play fast and loose with the rules because he has only his own movements to be aware of, apart from those of wind and water. But if two people are in a canoe, then beware, for if both are in unstable conditions and if both have contributed to a high C of G, the slightest movement of one can prove the undoing of the other and, of course, both.

It is, therefore, axiomatic that a bow paddler *always* kneel, and a stern paddler often do so, particularly when conditions dictate.

"So," you ask, "if a bow paddler always kneels, why in hell do they put a perfectly good usable seat in the bow?"

Easy: because a solo paddler invariably paddles stern first, and he *may* sit on the seat.

There is one manufacturer who ensures this cannot be done, by placing a thwart immediately abaft the front seat. The solo paddler (stern first) must always kneel.

This same manufacturer sells an incredible array of gadgetry for making canoes into catamarans, outriggers, motor boats, sail boats, and racing shells, obviously in complete ignorance of the intent of the canoe, and singlemindedly determined to sell his tin boats to people who didn't really want a canoe in the first place.

These are three basic positions for a rear or solo paddler (as opposed to only one for the bow):

- Sitting on the seat.
- Kneeling, rump against, but not on, the rear seat and feet tucked under, braced against the hull for stability.
- Kneeling, sitting on feet, forward of seat and not

touching it, anywhere between the seat and the center thwart, to the point where the knees are under the center thwart and the thwart is against the chest or stomach. This is the position in an empty canoe, paddled stern first, against a headwind. By moving forward and tipping the canoe gunwale down, apart from other salutary effects, the windage is reduced. It is to achieve this effect in part that the solo paddler goes stern first because the bow seat is already much closer to the center thwart than is the stern seat.

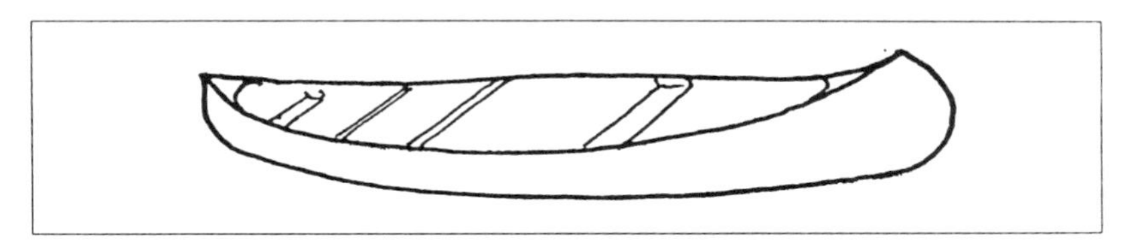

Depending on the ballast aboard, the rear or solo paddler sits on the seat with left buttock (if paddling on the left side), the left leg outstretched, and the right leg tucked back under the seat to lock himself to the canoe. The right knee may or may not touch the bottom of the canoe.

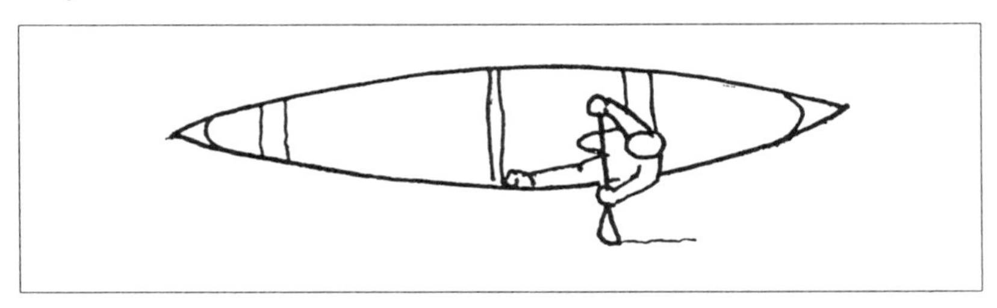

This last position is not to be confused with the left leg kneeling and right leg extended of the right-handed racing paddler. It is a relaxed, comfortable position for stable conditions when there is no great demand for power and when the boat is ballasted to provide stability.

When two paddlers are up and the boat is trimmed dead

level, they paddle in unison on opposite sides, and the bow sets the stroke.

When three paddlers are up, the middle kneels against the center thwart, paddling on the same side as the stern, and the bow sets the stroke.

A fourth would require #3 to move aft of center, paddling on the same side as bow, and #4 to paddle on the same side as the stern, forward of center.

"Well Okay" you concede, "but kneeling all day?" Paddlers don't have a monopoly on discomfort. Use a pad—a thin pad, that is. A boat cushion puts the center of gravity too high.

Passengers

Time was when every canoe was equipped with a fan-shaped back rest to be used by non-paddling passengers.

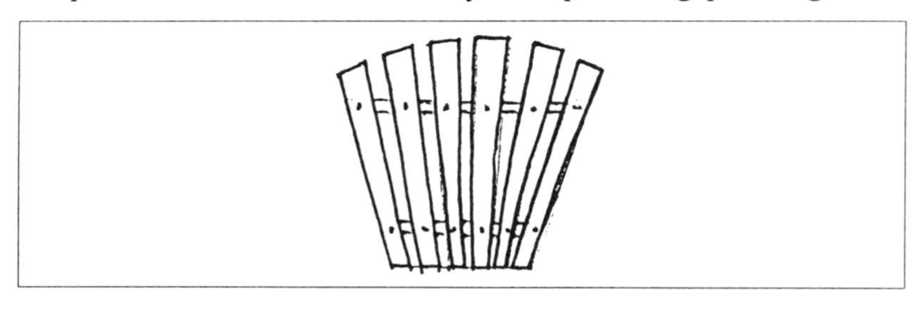

The classic picture was of a young swain taking his lady friend for a paddle, he sitting on the stern seat and she seated facing him on a cushion, against a back rest set against the bow seat.

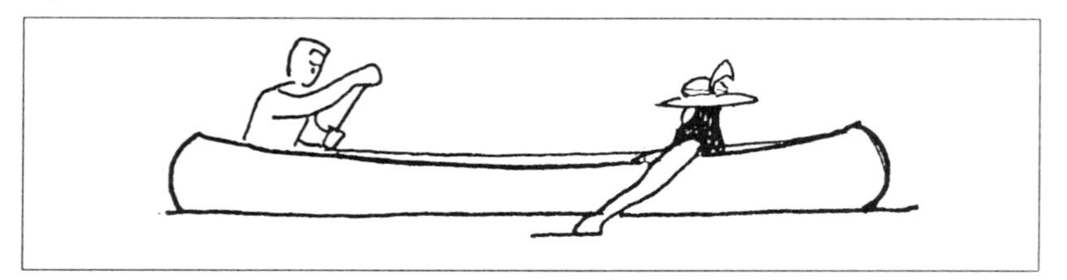

Certainly the back rest-cum-cushion idea was good, because the ribs of a canvas canoe were most uncomfortable. Nowadays there are no ribs in most canoes, but neither is there something to secure the bottom of the back rest. You win some, and you lose some!

But consider this. How could one have a real "hands-on" relationship with him in the stern, and her away up there in the bow?

Suppose she could manufacture a martini-shaker or manipulate a church key. How was she going to get the glass or bottle back to him anyway, without getting up and probably upsetting the whole act?

Well, try this:

> "Prepare to paddle stern first. Place the back rest and cushion against the center thwart, starboard side, so that passenger faces the rear. Help the lady into the boat and admonish her not to jiggle around too much until you get in, because she is sitting well to starboard, the right gunwale is well down, and you don't want to lose the six-pack.
>
> Ease yourself onto the bow seat facing forward (natch) and now adjust positions until the hull trims slightly down by the paddling side gunwale."

Now what do we have?

A well-trimmed boat, slightly down by the rear but not unacceptably so, and best of all, proximity. No problem with hands on here, passing the port, or any other little thing to be shared. Try it!

Canoe-Associated Equipment

Packs

Like almost everything else related to canoeing, a canoe pack is a compromise. In order to stow well in the canoe, it must be a soft pack, without frame or packboard. It therefore is not an ideal pack to carry.

The Woods #1 Special pack was designed for canoe work. It was heavy duck, well waterproofed, 24 inches x 20 inches x 6 inches, with wide leather shoulder straps. It came equipped with a tump, so that at least two packs could be carried simultaneously, one atop the other, if a canoe was not also carried. The tump could very conveniently be adapted to use on the canoe by lacings through the buckle holes at either end, fastened through the gunwale slots, adjusted, and tied.

Trip shirt

A heavy wool shirt is ideally suited to the canoeist's needs. Folded, it serves as a kneeling pad. Rolled and tied around the neck it provides a pad for carrying. It will shed water as well as many storm jackets without the clammy characteristics of the waterproof, and being wool, is still warm when thoroughly soaked.

Axe

The one indispensable item for the tripper or wilderness traveller is his axe. It should be a small axe, but not one of those one-handed shin splitters. About a 2½-pound head and a 24-inch helve is adequate.

Lashed under the gunwale with belt lacing, it is always easily available and, in case of mishap, is more likely to be retrievable if secured to the canoe than if in a pack.

With a good axe, one can make a new paddle, repair the canoe, make a whole new boat or raft if necessary, cut firewood, construct shelter, protect oneself, and generally construct anything needed. Without it, life could be extremely difficult.

An axe file (one side crosscut, other side bastard) and stone are essential to maintain the axe.

Wing nuts

There are many times when flies or mosquitoes can make sleep in the bush impossible unless one has a bug-proof shelter. The only way to escape these pests is to go far enough out on the water that they will not follow.

If one or more thwarts have had the nuts on the end bolts affixing them to the hull replaced with wing nuts, removal of the thwarts greatly facilitates sleeping in the bottom of the canoe. A canoe pack (empty) attached to the painter makes a satisfactory sea anchor under these circumstances.

Belt lacing

Time was that most machinery ran off a wide canvas belt, whether from the overhead drive shaft in a machine shop, or from the tractor flywheel to the threshing-machine.

These belts were joined at their ends by belt lacing, a tanned leather thong of indeterminate length, like a boot lace, but about twice as wide.

The one property that suited the belt lacing ideally for canoe painter, axe lashing, etc., was that a half hitch, under tension, would hold as well as a square knot or bowline.

Today, belt lacing is hard to find, but a good 72-inch boot lace of chrome-tanned leather will do almost as well.

A Stable Platform

As noted earlier, nothing can compare to a canoe for getting into the swamp. When the marsh grass is so high and thick that you can no longer paddle, you can still pull that sharp prow through what appears to be an impenetrable jungle.

After you get there, however, what can you do? Anyone who has tried to shoot from a canoe, or move around to take pictures knows the frustration of that unstable platform. And as for getting a muddy, stinking retriever in and out of a canoe, forget it!

Suppose your bag is photographing the mating habits of the early morning tadpole catcher, or ritual dance of the great horned bill edger, or mebbe you just want to slaughter a few innocent waterfowl: what do you do?

Before setting out, cut four (or more) willow poles 1½ to 2 inches in diameter and about the length of your boat. Sharpen one end, and when you arrive at the ideal spot for your blind, drive two poles well into the mud bottom, so that they cross just below the waterline.

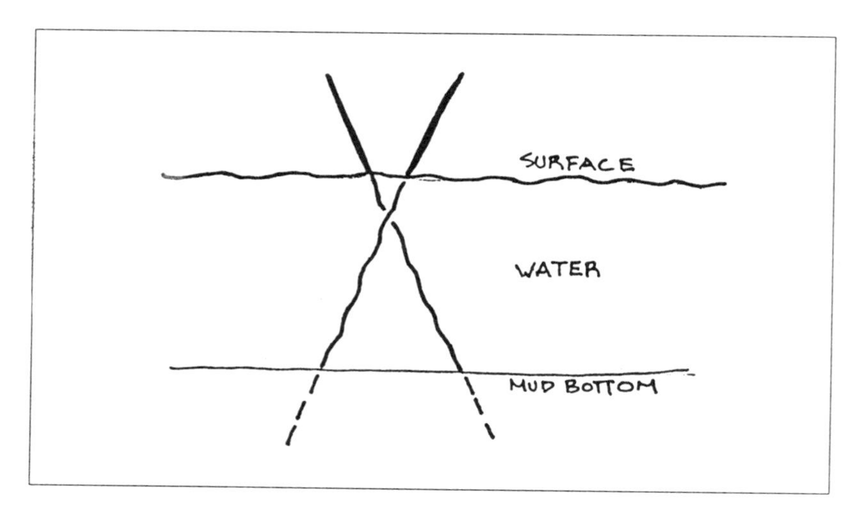

Manoeuvre the bow or stern into the cradle provided and lash the gunwales securely into the poles. Repeat with the other two poles for the other end of the boat.

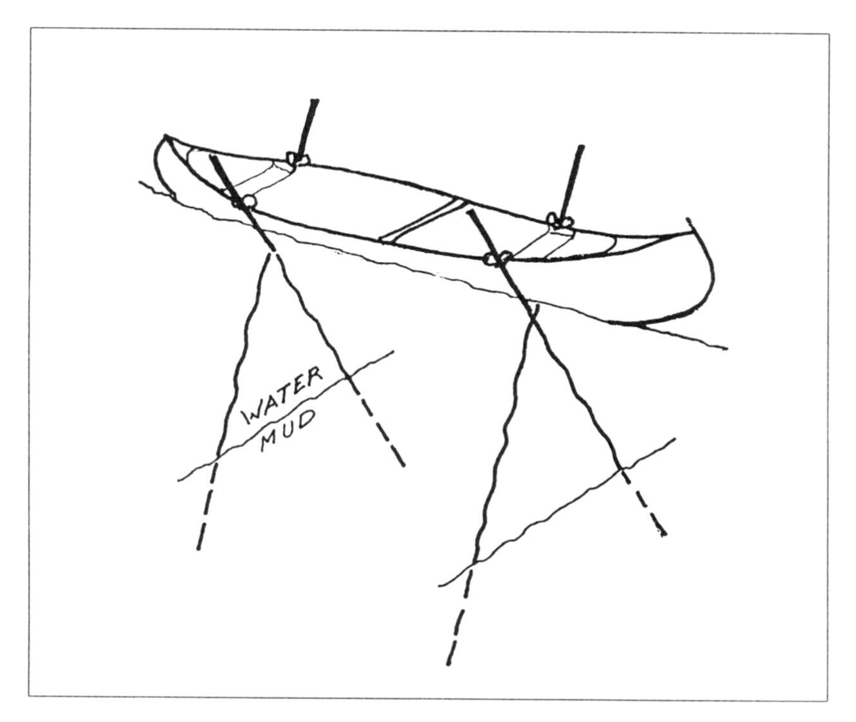

You will find that this platform is stable enough to shoot from (camera or gun) for one or more people, and you can work a dog very comfortably from it. Without a dog, retrieving would be awkward because you would have to continually untie the lashings.

If the poles are cut long enough, they also may be trimmed to make ideal supports for canopy, camouflage net, or whatever else your blind requires.

When finished for the day, leave the poles there for next time. They should last a whole season.

Safety afloat

"Were you in the boat when the boat tipped over?"

"No, I was in the water!"

One of the basic skills of the dinghy sailor is that of

learning to right his craft after dunking, and any worthwhile sail-training program will devote a considerable amount of time to the practice of this skill.

Sooner or later, almost everyone who paddles a lot will overturn a canoe. In the days of canvas canoes, the behaviour of a boat under these circumstances was fairly predictable because the whole structure was buoyant material. It was nevertheless a worthwhile exercise to dump the canoe in shallow water to experiment with the problem of refloating it.

Certain characteristics, like the extreme instability of the hull when totally or partially filled with water, the tremendous suction of an overturned hull when one tries to lift it, and the difficulties to be encountered in removing enough water in order that the remainder can be bailed out, all could be examined in relative comfort. So could the various facile formulae expounded by "experts" for coping with the situation after dumping.

With the proliferation of hulls made from non-buoyant material, experimentation of this nature becomes even more important. Most glass and metal canoes have some type of built-in flotation, but without experimentation under controlled conditions, it is difficult to predict how they will behave in an emergency.

Time was when only small children, rank novices, or non-swimmers wore life jackets when canoeing. The only life jackets available were bulky, cumbersome, and uncomfortable, and paddlers preferred to rely on the buoyancy of the canoe rather than be encumbered by such apparatus.

Today, there are flotation garments which are as comfortable to wear as a waistcoat, and there is no excuse for them not being worn at all times while on the water. Nevertheless, you and I know this will not happen.

First, review some of the caveats:

— If you must run white water, first unload your valuables and necessities, and wear a life jacket.
— For white water, if you have a canvas deck, use it. If you intend to do it often, get one.
— If in doubt, portage.
— Don't overload.
— Trim the craft carefully.
— Ensure dead ballast will not shift.
— Keep C of G low.
— Ensure paddlers are in stable, locked-in positions.
— Counsel passengers on the effect of the human head (20 pounds) suddenly swivelled around.
— Don't get broadside to large waves or swells.
— Stay close to shore if possible, preferably a windward shore (one from which the wind is coming), rather than a lee shore (one to which the wind is blowing).
— Cross large bodies of water with caution. It is sometimes preferable to have canoes towed or transported across large open bodies (No, Virginia, that is not cheating), if such a facility is available.
— Learn to read weather signs or interpret meteorological reports.
— Cross potentially dangerous open water in the early morning or late evening, when it is most likely to be calm.
— Travel with another boat, if possible, particularly on stretches of water that may be dangerous.
— Keep a bailer handy for the occasional big one that comes over the gunwales. A hat or shoe is better than nothing, but the tea pail can just as easily be left unpacked. Tie it in, though. It's of no use in the deep-six.
— Don't get caught by a big one with your paddle out

of the water. An immersed blade ensures that you can apply some righting moment to the hull.

— Shun round-bottomed canoes, old or new.
— The best way to really lower C of G is to lie down.

If calamity does strike:
First of all in non-threatening weather conditions:

— If wearing life jackets, try to right the canoe, bail out as much water as necessary, get aboard, and bail out the rest.
— If not wearing life jackets, find them, put them on, and then decide if you still have enough energy to bail the canoe, etc.
— If not wearing life jackets and they can't be found, stay with the canoe, don't try to bail it, and swim/drift it to shore.
— If you are lucky enough to be in the company of another canoe, hang on to him (ensuring you don't capsize him), and he can partially haul your canoe over his gunwale, dump the water, and help you reboard. Remember, though, one canoe overturned may be a problem; two canoes over may be a catastrophe.

If the weather conditions are threatening:

— If the waves, wind, and weather are the problems that caused the difficulty, and another boat is present, don't let him try to right your canoe, or even take you aboard, unless the water temperature is a threat to life. It is better to get to shore safely with one boat afloat than none, so hold onto his hull in a way not to threaten stability (for example, one man on either side of center thwart), proceed to shore, and leave your boat for the waves to bring along later.

— If one boat is alone and it was the elements that caused the accident, there is little likelihood of being able to bail or reboard the craft. Stay with the boat, and swim it to shore if possible.

But, in any case when alone, *stay with the boat—ALWAYS!*

A Final Word

If you happen to be the owner of a real "dog," don't despair. My first canoe was a classic, as dogs go, but I probably realized more pleasure from the ownership of that boat than any I have had since.

It may be with a little expert help, or luck, or both, you can remove that offensive keel. On a glass boat, perhaps the hull can even be rockered slightly by wedging apart at the center section the slot left by the removal of the keel before reglassing the bottom. Who knows?

If not, better luck next time. A good boat, though it may appear expensive, is an investment that will always pay dividends.

And in the meantime, whittle out a good paddle and center thwart, put some slotted gunwales on your boat, and learn how to paddle and carry.

Remember, it is not the various arm/hand/body movements that are important, it's the theory behind them. Your application of those principle may produce a style that bears little resemblance to that of the next fellow. No matter: it's results that count.

Long May Your Paddle Sing, And Sweetly!

Other Hancock House Titles

Robert Service
51/2 X 81/2, 64 pp. SC
ISBN 0-88839-223-0

Robert Service
51/2 X 81/2, 64 pp. SC
ISBN 0-88839-224-9

Jack London
51/2 X 81/2, 104 pp. SC
ISBN 0-88839-259-1

Chief Dan George and Helmut Hirnschall
51/2 X 81/2, 96 pp. SC
ISBN 0-88839-231-1

Chief Dan George and Helmut Hirnschall
51/2 X 81/2, 96 pp. SC
ISBN 0-88839-233-8

Mike Puhallo, Brian Brannon, and Wendy Liddle
51/2 X 81/2, 64 pp. SC
ISBN 0-88839-368-7

Robert F. Harrington
51/2 X 81/2, 96 pp. SC
ISBN 0-88839-367-9

pj johnson
51/2 X 81/2, 64 pp. SC
ISBN 0-88839-366-0

James and Susan Preyde
51/2 X 81/2, 96 pp. SC
ISBN 0-88839-362-8

All titles available from HANCOCK HOUSE PUBLISHERS, 1431 Harrison Ave., Blaine, WA 98230-5005
(604) 538-1114 Fax: (604) 538-2262 Mastercard, Visa, or Check accepted.